Ichiro Suzuki: Baseball's Most Valuable Player

Influential Asians

ICHIRO SUZUKI

Baseball's Most Valuable Player

David Aretha

Enslow Publishing
101 W. 23rd Street
Suite 240
New York, NY 10011
USA
enslow.com

Published in 2017 by Enslow Publishing, LLC.
101 W. 23rd Street, Suite 240, New York, NY 10011

Library of Congress Cataloging-in-Publication Data

Names: Aretha, David, author.
Title: Ichiro Suzuki : baseball's most valuable player / David Aretha.
Description: New York : Enslow Publishing, 2017. | Series: Influential Asians | Includes bibliographical references and index.
Identifiers: LCCN 2015050612 | ISBN 9780766079021 (Library Bound)
Subjects: LCSH: Suzuki, Ichiro, 1973---Juvenile literature. | Baseball players--Japan--Biography--Juvenile literature.
Classification: LCC GV865.S895 A74 2017 | DDC 796.357092--dc23
LC record available at http://lccn.loc.gov/2015050612

Printed in the United States of America

To Our Readers: We have done our best to make sure all websites in this book were active and appropriate when we went to press. However, the author and the publisher have no control over and assume no liability for the material available on those websites or on any websites they may link to. Any comments or suggestions can be sent by e-mail to customerservice@enslow.com.

Photo Credits: Cover, 10, 55, 59, 96, 99 Otto Greule Jr/Getty Images Sport/Getty Images; p. 6 Lisa Blumenfeld/Getty Images Sport/Getty; p. 9 DAN EVINE/AFP/Getty Images; p. 13 Carl Mydans/The LIFE Picture Collection/Getty Images; p. 18, 25, 27, 40, 47, 51 The Asahi Shimbun via Getty Images; p. 22 ぽこ太郎 /File:20111127 'Aikodai Meiden' High school Baseball Club at Meiji Jingu Stadium.JPG/Wikimedia Commons; p. 31 JiJi Press/AFP/Getty Images; p. 33 Hulton Archive/Getty Images; p. 44 Elsa/Getty Images Sport/Getty Images; p. 64, 67 DAN LEVINE/AFP/Getty Images; p. 74 PAUL BUCK/AFP/Getty Images; p. 76 Pilling/MLB Photos/Getty Images Sport/Getty Images; p. 82 Aflo Co. Ltd/Alamy Stock Photo; p. 86 Brad Mangin /Sports Illustrated/Getty Images; p. 89 Kyodo News/Newscom; p. 91 Pete Souza/The White House via Getty Images; p. 103 Mike Stobe/Getty Images Sport/Getty Images; p. 105 Brian Garfinkel/Getty Images Sport/Getty Images; p. 107 Adam Hunger/Getty Images Sport/Getty Images; p. 109 Mitchell Layton/Getty Images Sport/Getty Images

Contents

Ichiro Suzuki's record-breaking hitting record has made him a baseball legend.

Chapter 1

All Hail Ichiro

Never before in America had a man from Japan been so loved.

On October 1, 2004, Ichiro Suzuki strode to the batter's box at Safeco Field in Seattle. As he looked around, he saw 45,573 fans standing and cheering. Many were taking his picture. It was a clear, cool night, and excitement crackled like electricity through the ballpark.

Earlier in this game against Texas, Ichiro had ripped his 257th hit of the season. The accomplishment was phenomenal. Reaching just two hundred hits is an amazing feat, usually achieved by just several Major League Baseball (MLB) players per year. With hit number 257, Ichiro tied the major league record set by George Sisler way back in 1920.

Now it was the sixth inning, and Ichiro had a chance to break Sisler's record. Fans were on their feet, rooting for their Mariners hero. Ichiro stepped into the left-handed batter's box. The Japanese-born hitting star was a slender man of average height. He wore his black hair short, with long sideburns. He looked handsome in his white pants and dark blue Mariners jersey. On his back he wore the number 51 with the name "Ichiro" above. All other players in the majors had their last name on their uniform. In this regard (and many others), Ichiro was unique.

Against Rangers pitcher John Wasdin, Ichiro waved his black bat, waiting for the first pitch. In the stands, a woman stood before a sign that read "Ichiro! 257." She held the number 8 in her hand, anxious to paste it over the 7. In the first row sat Frances Sisler Drochelman, George Sisler's eighty-one-year-old daughter. Dressed sharply in a beige pantsuit, she stood arrow straight. While there to represent her father, she showed wonderful sportsmanship by clapping for the Mariners star.

As he waited on the 1–1 (one-ball, one-strike) pitch, Ichiro twirled his bat like an orchestra conductor does a baton. Wasdin wound and fired a pitch down the middle, and Ichiro honed in on it. He strode toward the ball, kept his head down, and banged a grounder between shortstop Michael Young and second base. "A ground ball back up the middle!" screamed Mariners announcer Dave Niehaus. "And there it is! He's the new all-time hit king in Major League history! Number 2-5-8! My, oh my!"[1]

As fans roared their lungs out, fireworks exploded above the huge "Safeco Field" sign in left field. The

The crowd in the stands at Safeco Field in Seattle erupted when Ichiro hit his 258th hit in 2004. The single broke the long-standing record, set by George Sisler in 1920.

scoreboard declared, “Ichiro Hit Count: 258.” Ichiro, who normally wore a serious expression during games, burst into a smile at first base. He took a deep breath, overwhelmed by the moment.

Since leaving Japan and joining the Mariners in 2001, Ichiro had been well liked and deeply respected. Now, during this celebratory moment, fans and players showered him with appreciation. Rangers first baseman Mark Teixeira shook his hand, and the Mariners players poured out of the dugout. Manager Bob Melvin was the first to greet Ichiro, embracing him with a hug. Then his teammates mobbed him, slapping him on the back and

Ichiro's teammates crowded around him to celebrate his remarkable achievement. The gracious star acknowledged his team, his fans, and George Sisler's daughter on this special night.

rubbing his fuzzy head. The roar continued, with one fan holding up a sign: "HITStory 2004."

"The usually . . . unemotional Ichiro Suzuki with a *huge* smile on his face . . . ," Niehaus exclaimed. "And with misty eyes, there is George Sisler's daughter clapping for the new hit champion of all time."[2]

With teammates still congratulating him, Ichiro broke away from the pack. He jogged across the field to Frances Sisler Drochelman and shook her hand. Appearing gracious and humble, he spoke a few words to her and she did the same. He smiled and bowed to her while holding her hand the whole time. As Ichiro shook the hands of her family members, Drochelman took off her eyeglasses. "You're darn right she's got tears in her eyes," Niehaus said.[3] Ichiro then acknowledged the Mariners fans, tipping his helmet to them several times. They responded with a deafening cheer.

"Tears Just Won't Stop Flowing"

Americans were not the only ones celebrating this moment. Back in Japan, fans still followed Ichiro with keen interest. It was around noon on Saturday, and fans gathered around televisions to watch their countryman break this extraordinary record. "He's incredible," said Shigeru Uchida, who watched the game at an electronics store in downtown Tokyo, Japan. "Baseball is America's

Most Hits in a Major League Season

Rank	Player	Hits	Year
1.	Ichiro Suzuki	262	2004
2.	George Sisler	257	1920
3.	Lefty O'Doul	254	1929
4.	Bill Terry	254	1930
5.	Al Simmons	253	1925
6.	Rogers Hornsby	250	1922
7.	Chuck Klein	250	1930
8.	Ty Cobb	248	1911
9.	George Sisler	246	1922
10.	Ichiro Suzuki	242	2001

game, and for him to go over there and do that is truly amazing."[4]

Nobuyuki Suzuki, Ichiro's father, also watched the game in Japan. He had worked with his son for thousands of hours, helping him become a champion hitter. "You can tell how happy and proud I am just by looking at me," he told a Japanese reporter. "The tears just won't stop flowing."[5]

Back in Seattle, the standing ovation lasted for a full five minutes. When Nobuyuki Suzuki and Frances Sisler were children, they could not have imagined such a scene. From 1941 to 1945, the United States and Japan had engaged in a horrific war. It began when Japan bombed Pearl Harbor in Hawaii. It ended when the United States dropped atomic bombs on Hiroshima and Nagasaki, Japan, killing roughly two hundred thousand people.

At the time, most Asian Americans lived in the West Coast states: California, Oregon, and Washington. That's because the quickest route from Asia to the United States was a boat ride across the Pacific Ocean to the shores of the West Coast. After America's war with Japan began, government leaders in Washington, DC, became suspicious of Japanese Americans. They worried that they would be loyal to Japan, not the United States. So, President Franklin Roosevelt ordered that Japanese Americans be sent to internment camps for the duration of the war.

More than one hundred thousand Japanese Americans were locked in these camps. Moreover, most of these families lost their homes and many of their possessions. It was a dark time in American history.

Thankfully, the United States and Japan have been at peace since the end of World War II. Gradually, Japanese Americans became more welcomed by their fellow citizens. For those who remembered Japanese internment, this was an emotional night. Americans were cheering for a Japanese native like never before.

After the game, Ichiro was still on an emotional high. "Through my career, I think this is the best moment," he said through an interpreter. "I can't really put it into words . . . I think that's the most emotional I've ever gotten in my life."[6]

The United States has had a complicated history with Japan. During World War II, the US government shuttled Americans of Japanese ancestry into internment camps.

Mariners manager Bob Melvin, who would be fired three days later, at least left with this wonderful memory. "*Goosebumps* aren't even the right word," Melvin said. "That second hit almost brought tears to my eyes . . . If you're talking about sending a guy up for a hit, this guy is the best ever."[7]

Drochelman also talked to the press after the historic game. "My father would have been delighted," she said. "He would be so happy to know such a fine young man was doing so well."[8]

In Japan, Prime Minister Junichiro Koizumi expressed his pride in Ichiro. "I would like to give him my heartfelt congratulations," he said. "He has made extra efforts in addition to having a natural gift."[9]

Ichiro's "extra efforts" had been extraordinary. As a child, he practiced obsessively with his father, hitting hundreds of balls every day of the year. As a professional, he placed his bats in a special "humidor" so that the wood would not get too hard or too soft. Away from the field, he dressed in flashy clothes and yet craved his privacy. He broke records of long-deceased heroes, then visited their gravesites with flowers. Jerry Brewer of the *Vancouver Sun* called Ichiro a "mysterious star," a "dynamo of habit," and a "solitary baseball savant," meaning a baseball genius.[10]

Ichiro began making those "extra efforts" as a small boy in Toyoyama, Japan. He received his first baseball mitt at age three, and at age six he launched his organized-baseball career. He was on his way to becoming the greatest Asian baseball player who ever lived.

Chapter 2

A Million Swings

As a seven-year-old boy in Japan, Ichiro starred on a youth baseball team. He had played ball with his dad, Nobuyuki, for several years, but now, at age seven, the boy wanted to get serious about his craft. He asked his father if he could teach him how to play the game properly. Nobuyuki responded with his own question: Can you promise to practice every day, without exception? Yes, the slender child promised. "Good, then," his father said. "We have a deal. Make sure you keep your end of it."[1]

Little Ichiro didn't realize it, but he had signed his life away to baseball. For 360 days or so per year, year after year, the father would practice with his son for hours each day. Ichiro would hit about two hundred balls after school, then another three hundred in the evening. That didn't include the running, throwing, pitching, and fielding that he was forced to do. Nobuyuki, it seemed, was on a mission to turn his son into a great professional ballplayer.

In later years, Nobuyuki said the marathon practices were "fun for both of us." Ichiro denied that claim. "It might have been for him," he said, "but for me it . . . bordered on hazing and I suffered a lot. But I also couldn't say no to him. He was doing his utmost to help me."[2]

It is not uncommon for fathers to push their sons hard in athletics. Critics of this approach wonder if the men do so for the benefit of their child or to fulfill their fantasy of seeing their son succeed in sports. With Nobuyuki, it's difficult to determine his motive. But it's clear that the man was obsessed.

Few Americans have gotten close enough to Ichiro to learn about his childhood. Author Robert Whiting is an exception. Much of the insight provided in this chapter comes from his revealing book *The Meaning of Ichiro: The New Wave from Japan and the Transformation of Our National Pastime*, published in 2004.

Son of the "3:30 Man"

Nobuyuki Suzuki and his wife, Yoshie, lived in Toyoyama, a suburb of the industrial city of Nagoya. Nobuyuki managed a small electrical parts factory, but his real love was baseball. Although he never pushed the game onto their oldest son, Kazuyasu, he did with their other child.

Yoshie gave birth to Ichiro on October 22, 1973. His name means "number one son"—another apparent slight to Kazuyasu. When Ichiro was three, Nobuyuki bought him the most expensive glove available, made of shiny red leather. It cost him half a month's wages, angering Yoshie. But for Nobuyuki, a boy couldn't achieve greatness without the finest tools. Father and son played catch in the backyard every day. Each evening, Dad made sure Ichiro cleaned and oiled his glove.

A year or two after Ichiro made his commitment to practicing, Nobuyuki's new life began. Every day, he left work at 3:30 p.m., prompting local folks to call him the "3:30 Man." He would meet Ichiro after school, and the two would head to the nearby baseball diamond. That was the setting for their legendary practices. Ichiro would jog, play catch, throw dozens of pitches from the mound, and make long throws. He batted off a tee and hit approximately two hundred pitches that his father threw to him. After that, Dad hit at least a hundred balls to him in the infield and outfield. Nobuyuki was careful not to praise his son, but he often bought him ice cream on the way home.

Ichiro's busy day was far from over. After dinner and homework, father and son headed to the Airport Batting Center, where Ichiro took 250 to 300 swings against the pitching machine. Dad made sure they were quality at-bats. He stood behind the netting and reprimanded his son if he swung at a pitch that was outside the strike zone.

Nobuyuki taught Ichiro to bat left-handed because of its two advantages. First, most pitchers are right-handed.

Even when Ichiro didn't feel like it, his father trained him relentlessly. Nobuyuki Suzuki taught his son the value of discipline and practice.

It's easier for left-handed hitters to hit against righties because of the angle that the right-hander throws from. Second, it's a closer run to first for a left-handed hitter. Nobuyuki envisioned Ichiro—who was extremely fast—beating out bunts and infield hits.

The Suzukis often stayed until the batting cages closed at 11 p.m. After they arrived home, Nobuyuki routinely massaged Ichiro's feet, believing that healthy feet were important for a healthy body. The next day, the routine would begin again.

Apparently, Nobuyuki's intense passion for baseball was not utterly abnormal for a Japanese man. "In our generation, baseball was huge," said Hide Sueyashi, a Japanese native who worked in scouting for the Seattle Mariners. "They would work in the daytime, then watch games in the evening. They would laugh or cry for their team if they won or lost. It was always a father's dream for his boy to be a baseball player."[3]

Get Up, Ichiro

Every human being deserves a day of rest, but Nobuyuki wouldn't allow it. They played in the heat of summer, when temperatures soared above ninety degrees Fahrenheit. They toiled in the depths of winter, with temperatures dipping into the thirties. When Ichiro hit the ball on a frigid day, he would feel a sting in his hands.

Sometimes, Ichiro rebelled against the endless, daily practices. He would declare that he wouldn't go—that he wanted to play with his friends instead—but his dad insisted he practice. At times, Ichiro would sit on the ball field's grass and refuse to move. One day, his father responded to this sit-down strike by firing balls hard at his son. Ichiro reacted by catching some with his glove and trying to dodge the others.

The practices continued, of course, and even included the "life or death" batting drill. In this routine, Nobuyuki put his own well-being on the line. He stood close to Ichiro and fired pitches hard. He instructed his son to rip the pitches to the right or left—and not drill him with a line drive.

All the while, Ichiro developed an unorthodox swing. Like a golfer (which his father was), he shifted his whole body weight into the pitch. His body moved forward and his bat would follow on a level plane. Though Ichiro was a line drive hitter, the momentum of his body helped him hit the ball a long way. (In the major leagues, the short, skinny player would hit over one hundred home runs.)

Focused on Success

Despite the insanely long practices, Ichiro appeared to be a regular kid. He did well in school and wore braces on his teeth. On nonschool days, he played with toys (Transformers) and video games (Nintendo). Childhood photos show him smiling and enjoying nonbaseball activities, including riding a horse. Besides practicing with his father, Ichiro played youth league ball, and of course he excelled. He began as a six-year-old in a league meant for ages eight and nine. He eventually earned the nickname "*Baz*," which meant a fast runner.

In junior high school, Ichiro's baseball routine changed. He joined his school team and was trained by his coach, although Dad attended all of the team's practices. He told the coach not to mess with Ichiro's swing and never to praise him. After dinner, Nobuyuki and Ichiro went to the batting cages. The boy then went home and did his homework, often staying up until 2 a.m. In the classroom, he often dozed off.

Despite the exhausting schedule, Ichiro liked the path he was on. At age twelve, he wrote the following essay.

> My dream when I grow up is to be a first-class professional baseball player . . . I have the confidence to do the necessary practice to reach that goal. I started practicing from age three. From the age of nine I practiced baseball 360 out of 365 days a year and I practiced hard. I only had five to six hours a year to play with my friends. That's how much I practiced. So I think I can surely become a pro. I will play in junior high school and high school. When I graduate I will enter the pros. My dream is to join the Seibu Lions or the Chunichi Dragons. My goal is a contract signing bonus of 100 million yen.[4]

Today, 100 million yen equals about $820,000. Ichiro had lofty ambitions, but he greatly exceeded them. In the major leagues alone, he has earned more than $150 million in salary.

The Rigors of High School

In his three years of junior high, Ichiro starred on the diamond and excelled in school. He then attended Aikodai Meiden Koko in Nagoya, a school known for its outstanding baseball program. The Japanese take high school baseball much more seriously than Americans do. Ichiro was one of fifty-one players in the baseball program, and they lived in the Meiden baseball dormitory eleven months of the year (excluding January). The modern, three-story dorm included a kitchen and laundry room on the first floor, bunk beds on the second, and a workout room on the third.

The baseball program at Meiden resembled the military. Focus was on hard work, discipline, honor, and the respect of elders—traits that are valued and emphasized in Japanese culture. At Meiden, only the top seventeen players could practice every day. Practice

The Aikodai Meiden school is still known for its outstanding baseball program. At Meiden, Ichiro further developed his discipline and devotion to the game of baseball.

lasted from 3:30 to 8 p.m., with batting practice later in the evening. The other thirty-four players had to do lowly chores, such as cooking and laundry, while respecting the elder players.

Those who offended a senior player could be punished. One such punishment was to sit atop a garbage can, with legs tucked underneath—a painful experience. What kind of offense did a player have to commit to be humiliated like that? "You name it," Ichiro said. "You have a bad attitude, or didn't rinse the rice properly before you cooked it. Once I remember they caught me eating a soft ice cream cone I'd gone out to buy, and it was up on the garbage can for me."[5]

In his first year at the three-year school, Ichiro was among the bottom thirty-four. The next year, as a junior, he cracked the top seventeen. For these "lucky" few, practice was grueling. They ran for miles each day, and they endured excruciating drills that built muscles and character. Players threw car tires and batted against Wiffle balls with a heavy shovel. Ichiro would grow to be just five-foot-nine (175 centimeters), and in high school he weighed just 120 pounds (about 54 kilograms). But he developed extraordinary strength in his slender muscles.

Ichiro found the experience extremely difficult, but he remained completely focused on his baseball tasks. The same couldn't be said for his schoolwork. He didn't study like he had in junior high, and he often snoozed in class. While he aimed to become a professional baseball player, Ichiro had to really excel to overcome his perceived liability: his tiny frame. Even in Japan, where players were smaller than in the United States, 120-pounders (54 kg) like Ichiro just didn't exist.

But Ichiro was one mighty mite. By his senior year, he shined as the best player on his team—as a hitter, pitcher, base stealer, and outfielder. In his career at Meiden, he cracked .505, belted 19 home runs, and stole 131 bases. Ichiro, who from a young age wrote the word *Concentration* on his mitt, focused intensely at the plate. In 536 high school at-bats, he struck out only ten times. Never once did he swing and miss for strike three. His father may have correlated his low strikeout rate to their days at the airport batting cages, when he reprimanded his son for swinging at nonstrikes.

One of the few pitchers who could have struck out Ichiro was he himself. The little right-hander packed a whistling fastball (93 miles per hour/150 kilometers) and an effective curveball.[6] Ichiro's pitching career ended after he hurt his arm during a bicycle accident.

Showcasing His Talents

Then as now, Japanese high school baseball teams played in the Koshein national tournaments, held in the spring and summer. Japanese fans are as nutty for these two tourneys as Americans are for the National Collegiate Athletic Association (NCAA) basketball tournament. Bands and cheerleaders support their schools. While thousands of high schools participate in the early rounds of the summer tournament, only forty-nine advance to the grand event. It's held in Koshein Stadium, home of

Ichiro was starting pitcher at Aikodai Meiden during the National High School Baseball Invitational Tournament in 1991.

professional Hanshin Tigers. The stadium seats fifty-five thousand, with stands that sweep majestically high.

Meiden participated in the Koshein tournament in the summer of his second year and the spring of his third. Meiden lost in the first round both times, and Ichiro was disappointed in his performances. "Knowing that it was broadcast live on TV made me tense up," he said.[7]

As huge as the Koshein tournament was, Ichiro geared up more for the summer prefectural tournament of his senior season. He knew this was his last chance to showcase his talents to professional scouts. His goal? To bat 1.000. "That's right," he said. "Not to ground out or fly out even once."[8] Apparently, striking out didn't even enter his mind. Though he didn't bat 1.000, he ripped a robust .750.

By the time of the professional player draft in November 1991, Ichiro weighed just 124 pounds (56 kg). However, his skill set and high school performances definitely intrigued scouts. His line drive stroke, batting eye, foot speed, outfield defense, and arm were all extraordinary. Based on testing by university researchers, he also possessed another important trait: the ability to stay calm under pressure. Their studies of brain wave activity revealed he was far more relaxed than fellow players, including during the national baseball tournament.[9]

Taking all factors into consideration, the Orix BlueWave drafted Ichiro in the fourth and final round of the Nippon Professional Baseball (NPB) draft. The NPB

In 1991, the Orix BlueWave drafted Ichiro onto its team. The young and scrappy player was on his way to achieving his childhood goals.

is the equivalent of America's Major League Baseball (MLB). It's comprised of two leagues, the Pacific and Central, just like MLB includes the American League (AL) and the National League (NL). Orix played in the Pacific League, which also included the Seibu Lions—one of the two teams Ichiro had wanted to play for as a kid. His other favorite team, the Chunichi Dragons, toiled in the Central League in nearby Nagoya.

Ironically, Orix was the only team to take Ichiro seriously as an outfielder. Other teams considered drafting him as a pitcher, despite his arm injury. In many scouts' minds, Ichiro's unorthodox swing, as well as his small size, wouldn't translate well to the pros.

Boy, were they wrong! Although he might have looked like a batboy, Ichiro was on the verge of taking professional baseball by storm. His years of endless batting practice, which included more than a million swings, were about to pay off—big-time.

Chapter 3

The "Man" in Japan

At age eighteen, Ichiro prepared to move far away from home. The Orix BlueWave played in the Japanese city of Kobe, more than two hundred miles (322 km) west of Ichiro's hometown. Kobe, with a current population of over 1.5 million, is known for its beef—and for being the inspiration for basketball star Kobe Bryant's first name. Ichiro didn't care where it was located. He was just focused on playing baseball.

When he arrived in Orix and saw the BlueWave, Ichiro did not feel intimidated. In the book *Ichiro on Ichiro*, he recalled examining a player named Punch Sato. "His defense wasn't anything special, and he wasn't a fast runner. I figured that at this rate I should be able to play on a Japanese major league team."[1]

Ichiro didn't expect to play in the majors right away. He figured he'd need a couple of years in the minors, which is where he began in 1992. Immediately, he showcased his line drive stroke with the minor league BlueWave. In fifty-eight games, he ripped .366, which happened to match the MLB career record held by Ty Cobb. Like the legendary outfielder, Ichiro wreaked havoc on the bases as well as at the plate, stealing 10 bases and legging out 4 triples. The little guy even socked 3 home runs.

In July 1992, Ichiro shared an experience with another all-time great outfielder: Willie Mays. Back in May 1951, Mays was hitting .477 for the minor league Minneapolis Millers. The New York Giants knew the kid was ready for the majors, so they called him up. Mays didn't want to go, saying he wasn't good enough yet. The same thing happened with Ichiro.

That July, "a team staffer called my room in the dorm and said, 'Tomorrow you're on the big-league roster.' But I told him, 'It's a little too soon; I'm fine staying on the minor league team.' 'Just do it,' he said."[2]

Ichiro was half right. In forty games for the Orix major league team, he batted .253, which was so-so for a veteran but extraordinary for an eighteen-year-old. In those forty games, he managed only 95 at-bats. This indicates that he was often used as a pinch hitter, pinch runner, and/or a defensive replacement.

In 1993, Ichiro experienced failure on the diamond for the first time in his life—and arguably the only time. Three times he was promoted to the major league team that year, and three times he was demoted. In forty-three games for Orix, he batted just .188. The team's batting coach believed that Ichiro's hitting mechanics were the

Ichiro was so successful in the minors that he was called to the majors. But he was wasn't quite ready for the big leagues.

problem. He wanted to work with the young hitter, but Ichiro refused. As Nobuyuki used to say, no one should monkey with Ichiro's swing. Orix's manager, Shozo Doi, also insisted that Ichiro change his swing. Because he refused to listen to his elder—an unusual show of defiance by a young Japanese player—the team demoted him for the third time that season.

It could be that Ichiro just didn't get a chance to get in a groove. In those forty-three games, he tallied just 64 at-bats. In the minors that year, he played regularly and continued to rip. In forty-eight games, he batted 186 times and stroked .371 with 8 home runs.

Entering 1994, Ichiro faced a crossroads. The twenty-year-old seemed too good for the minors but not good enough for the majors. As it turned out, Ichiro would play seven full seasons with Orix (1994 to 2000), never again returning to the minor leagues.

The Rich History of Japanese Baseball

After World War II, the Japanese rebuilt their economy and adopted many aspects of Western culture, such as clothes, food, and television. Today, many Americans believe that the Japanese also adopted baseball around this time, but it's not true. The Japanese did learn the game from Americans, but they did so back around 1870. At the time, an American professor named Horace Wilson introduced the sport while teaching at a Japanese university.

The sport became popular at the collegiate and high school levels, with the first Koshien (national high school tournament) beginning in 1915. In 1934, American stars including Babe Ruth and Lou Gehrig played against Japanese players in Japan. Though the Americans dominated, pitcher Eiji Sawamura managed to strike out Ruth and Gehrig. Inspired by these contests, Japanese baseball enthusiasts started the country's first professional league two years later.

Nippon Professional Baseball, similar in structure to MLB, began in 1949. The NPB included the Central League and Pacific League, and the winners of each faced each other in the Japan Series—a takeoff of the World Series. Teams were named after corporations, not cities. Some teams took their nicknames from the major league

The Japanese have a long and rich history with the game of baseball. The sport was introduced to Japan in the nineteenth century but didn't become a professional sport until 1949.

clubs, including the Yamiuri Giants, Osaka Tigers, and Nishi Nippon Pirates. Others had distinctly Japanese names, such as the Chunichi Dragons.

The Giants are like the New York Yankees of the NPB. Not only have they played in Japan's largest city, Tokyo, but they have won the Japan Series the most times: twenty-two. From 1959 to 1980, the Giants featured the Babe Ruth of Japan. Sadaharu Oh blasted 868 home runs, with a high of 55 in 1964.

Slightly Different from MLB

From an American perspective, the NPB is fascinating because it is similar to major league ball but with a few differences. Starting with the actual baseball, the Japanese ball is slightly smaller and tighter than the American ball. The strike zone is a little narrower than the American zone. In Japan, the distance to the fences is shorter and so are the players. The average height of a Japanese man is five feet seven inches (170 cm), three inches shorter than the typical American man. Even the leagues are smaller. The Central and Pacific Leagues include just six teams apiece. Their seasons are only 143 games, compared to 162 in the major leagues.

In MLB, the American League includes a designated hitter (DH) and the National League does not use it. Interestingly, the Pacific League uses the DH and the Central League lets the pitcher bat. In Japan, a regular season game that is tied after 12 innings is declared a tie. Japanese teams have twenty-five-man rosters, like MLB teams do, but they limit the number of foreign-

The Babe Ruth of Japan

In the 1970s, two sluggers shook the world with their historic home runs. In 1974, Hank Aaron of the Atlanta Braves broke Babe Ruth's major league record of 714 home runs. Four years later in Japan, an overflow crowd of fifty-five thousand at Korakuen Stadium in Tokyo witnessed history. Sadaharu Oh, age thirty-eight, belted a homer to right field, becoming the first professional player to reach 800 home runs. Giants fans went crazy. When Oh reached home plate, a young woman draped a lei around his neck and handed him a giant baseball.

A left-handed hitter, Oh stood just five feet ten inches. But with a high front leg kick and a flawless swing, he clobbered 868 home runs for Yomiuri from 1959 through 1980. "I had strong legs that would have made me a good sumo wrestler and I used that to my advantage, but my home runs were achieved by technique," he said.

Oh knocked 40 homers or more thirteen times, with a high of 55 in 1964. He won nine Central League MVP Awards and took the Giants to eleven Japan Series titles—including nine straight from 1965 to 1973. He was Japan's most celebrated player until the 1990s, when a guy named Ichiro came along.

born players to four for each team. The NBP does not want teams to load up on American players. The quality of play is considered better in Major League Baseball, but not by much. Some experts say that NBP players are superior to those in Triple-A, the highest level of play in MLB's minor leagues.

More than fifty Japanese-born players have played in America's major leagues, most of whom have been pitchers. Masanori Murakami was the first Japan native to play in the majors, pitching for the San Francisco Giants in 1964. Through 2015, a dozen Japanese natives were selected to the MLB All-Star Game. Multiple selections included Ichiro (ten All-Star Games), strikeout ace Yu Darvish (three), control pitcher Kazuhiro Sasaki (two), and slugger Hideki Matsui (two). Many, many other Japanese players were good enough to play major league ball in the United States. They just chose not to.

Besides the rule differences between NPB and MLB, traditions are different, too. NPB teams employ six starting pitchers, as opposed to the five-man rotations in the United States. Japanese pitchers tend to throw more pitches per start as well as a large variety of breaking pitches, putting a great deal of stress on their arms. As such, their starters pitch only about once per week. Respect is highly stressed in Japanese society, including in baseball. If a pitcher hits a batter with a pitch, he is expected to tip his cap to the batter. In Japan, fights among players are unheard of.

In Japan, professional baseball contests include all the fanfare of American college football games. Each team has its own cheering section, where fans pound drums, blow horns, wave flags and banners, and yell through megaphones. They pump their fists, chant, and sing their team's fight song.

Breakout Season

The Orix team motto was "Get power! Be excited." For seven full seasons, the Orix BlueWave cheering section hooted, hollered, and sang for Ichiro. His breakout season arrived in 1994. Manager Shozo Doi, who had clashed with Ichiro in 1993, was no longer with the team. Akiri Ogi, an easygoing guy who loved to have a good time, became the new skipper. He inserted Ichiro into the starting lineup and let him hit however he darn-well pleased. The young player responded with one of the greatest seasons in Pacific League history.

Due to the 130-game schedule, the Pacific League record for hits in a season was only 191. Ichiro broke that mark on September 14, 1994, and he finished the season with 210 hits. His .385 batting average also set a league record, and in one stretch he reached base in sixty-nine consecutive games. He stole 29 bases and, thanks to more muscle and weight, he belted 13 home runs. He was named the league's Most Valuable Player (MVP) and earned a Gold Glove Award for the first of seven straight seasons. The award honored the best defensive NPB players at each position.

As mentioned, the NPB was nearly as competitive as the major leagues. To illustrate, Ichiro had a teammate that year named Francisco Cabrera. In his five previous seasons, all with MLB's Atlanta Braves, Cabrera had batted a combined .254. With the Oriz in 1994, he hit .237. It's not inconceivable, then, that Ichiro could have hit around .385 in the majors that year.

Suzuki is the second most common surname in Japan. So that their young star would stand out to fans, the BlueWave promoted him simply as Ichiro. He resisted the special treatment at first, but then came to accept it. That's the name that appeared on the back of his jersey, above the number 51.

Late in the 1994 season, American fans began to hear about Ichiro. Major league players went on strike beginning August 12, and no games were played after that. Even the playoffs and World Series were canceled. Thus, newspaper editors were looking for any good baseball story they could find to fill their sports sections. In October, the *Washington Post* found a great story in Ichiro.

The article recounted Ichiro's history as well as his swing: "During the pitcher's windup, Ichiro picks up his front leg and swings it like a long, slow pendulum back toward the catcher. Thus he is virtually tottering on one foot, weight far back, bat cocked, as the pitch approaches the plate. Then there's a blinding swing, a ferocious whack!, and the ball streaks like a bullet between second and short for another base hit."

The article stated that Ichiro still lived in a small room in an Orix corporate dorm and described him (correctly) as polite and serious. Unlike other players, he didn't clap or get excited after scoring a run. The *Post* quoted Cabrera: "Ichiro, he can hit anywhere. I'd say the person he most reminds me of is Tony Gwynn. Both of them have that quick swing and that fast takeoff toward first. They're already running when they hit the ball." Cabrera added that Ichiro liked to wear MLB team jerseys and that he was interested in one day playing in the United States.[3]

Doing It for Kobe

Fans in Kobe hailed Ichiro as a hero, and he made extra money by endorsing various products. On January 17, 1995, none of that matter. A major earthquake struck Kobe, killing more than four thousand people in the city and over six thousand in the region. Hundreds of thousands were left homeless. Ichiro was on the fourth floor of his dorm; his TV fell over and he feared that his building would crumble. Shaken physically and emotionally, Ichiro and his teammates donated money to help the victims. During the upcoming season, they wore patches on their jerseys that read "Let's Do It for Kobe."

The BlueWave reflected the city's spirit by winning the Pacific League title. Ichiro led the league in batting (.342), stolen bases (49), and runs batted in (RBIs) (80). Physically stronger, he belted 25 home runs. In the Japan Series, he socked a homer in the fifth and final game, though the Yakult Swallows took the series. Ichiro again won the Pacific League MVP Award.

Meanwhile, a Japanese pitcher dominated headlines in 1995. NPB players were supposed to play with their teams for their first ten seasons, but Hideo Nomo's lawyer found a loophole in his contract. Nomo fulfilled his dream of playing in the United States, finding glory

Ichiro Suzuki and his Orix BlueWave teammates celebrate after winning the Pacific League in 1995. Unfortunately, the team lost the Japan Series, but Ichiro was named Pacific League MVP.

with the Los Angeles Dodgers. Known as "The Tornado" due to his twisty windup and blazing fastball, Nomo went 13–6 with a 2.54 earned runs average (ERA) as a Dodgers rookie in 1995. He led the National League in strikeouts (236), made the All-Star team, and won the NL Rookie of the Year Award. Japanese fans followed his games on television, and the NPB began to rethink their binding contracts. Later in the decade, the league would make it easier for Japanese players to play in the United States.

In 1996, the *Toronto Globe and Mail* speculated that Ichiro might be the next great Japanese player to come to the United States. The newspaper referred to him as "the current poster boy of Japanese baseball. He's flirted with a .400 average much of his career, steals bases, makes girls blush and sells just about every consumer product in Japan."[4]

Indeed, Ichiro was the most popular player in Japan, as his image graced billboards throughout the country. All the while, Nobuyuki delighted in his son's glory. Dad often made the long drive to Kobe, where he signed autographs and talked to reporters. In 1996, Ichiro won another batting title (.356) and his third (and final) Pacific League MVP Award. He even pitched to a batter in an all-star game between the Pacific League and Central League. The crowd cheered like crazy during his warm-up tosses, then went wild when he induced a groundout.[5]

Later in the year, Ichiro sparked Orix to the Japan Series, and this time they prevailed, winning the clinching Game 5 in Kobe. That November, Ichiro and a team of Japanese stars faced MLB greats, including Cal Ripken, Pedro Martinez, Alex Rodriguez, and Mike Piazza. Throughout the multicity exhibition series, American players raved about the speedy little line drive hitter, who batted .636 in 11 at-bats. "The excitement I felt in that series was definitely a turning point," he said. "[T]he Majors became a definite goal of mine."[6]

After the season, Orix offered Ichiro a one-year contract worth the equivalent of $2 million. He accepted, even though many older players in the league earned much more. Though the best player in Japan, Ichiro said he shouldn't make what the more established players were earning. He came across as genuinely humble and respectful. Yet another psychological element may explain why he settled for a lower-than-expected salary.

Throughout his career, Ichiro held himself to extremely high standards. When he didn't reach them, he felt disappointed with himself, and even depressed. When Mike Piazza told him that he could play in the majors, Ichiro said, "I probably would be the bat boy."[7] Humility or self-loathing? It was hard to tell with Ichiro, but his upbringing was probably a factor. "Never praise him," his father had told his coaches.

Roll Him Up in Carpet

As Japan's greatest baseball player, Ichiro experienced the highs and lows of fame. Besides his brilliant all-around play, he was young, hip, and handsome—a "rock star" in cleats. He could not go out in public without being mobbed by autograph seekers and other fans. On the street, he wore baggy pants, cool sunglasses, and caps tilted sideways. He also developed a line of clothing, which became a huge seller.

On a trip to Kobe late in Ichiro's Pacific League career, *Sports Illustrated* writer Michael Farber entered a BlueWave souvenir store. There, he wrote, were "Ichiro cups, key chains, baseballs, action figures, jerseys, T-shirts, posters, cell-phone headsets, wristbands, stickers, calendars, notebooks, biographies, pins, memo pads, good-luck symbols, towels, postcards and flags."[8]

Despite this celebrity image, Ichiro remained an "old soul." He grew *bonsai* trees and enjoyed alone time with his dog and tropical fish. A thoughtful man, he stared at his fish tank for long stretches, achieving an inner peace and tranquility. While adored by teenage girls, he developed a long-term relationship with a professional woman who was seven years his senior. Yumiko Fukushima, whom he began dating in 1997, was a well-known sportscaster in Japan.

This couple couldn't be seen in public without sparking a mob scene. One time, Ichiro evaded the press by having his friends roll him up in a carpet. They took him in a pickup truck to meet Yumiko.[9] Though both were celebrities, Ichiro and Yumiko forged a strong personal relationship. "I could be myself with her, completely," Ichiro said. "And she said the same thing. Another big factor was that she got along really well with my parents."[10] In the fall of 1998, they got engaged.

Being Best Isn't Good Enough

From 1997 to 1999, Ichiro continued to roll. He stretched his batting title streak to six by ripping .345, .358, and .343 (in a season shortened by a broken wrist). He clubbed 17, 13, and 21 homers while stealing 39, 11, and 12 bases. During a stretch in 1997, he made a record 216 consecutive plate appearances without striking out.

Despite his consistent excellence, Ichiro continued to mentally punish himself. "The four years '95 to '98, it was a constant struggle to get to the top," he revealed in *Ichiro on Ichiro*. "I don't think many people were aware of this,

As Ichiro's star rose, he attracted the attention of many young women. Instead of playing the field, he married Yumiko Fukushima.

though. People kept praising me, saying how great my batting was . . . but those numbers hid the deep despair I was secretly feeling over my batting . . . more often than not I was very self-critical and struggled terribly. During the seven years I played for Orix, I often felt lost and, deep down, never really believed in my abilities as a ballplayer."[11]

The interviewer for the book, Narumi Komatsu, persistently questioned Ichiro on this topic. How could the best hitter in Asia feel he was failing at his craft? Was he battling issues that were broader and deeper than hitting, such as depression? No, said Ichiro. "If this was just a question of psychological turmoil or depression I think I could have handled it. But I was struggling with technical aspects of hitting, and I couldn't find any way to switch gears to be more positive."[12] He then delved into a long discussion about the technical aspects of hitting.

In MLB, hitters typically feel miserable when they're struggling at the plate. But never has a perennial batting champion been known to feel frustrated and depressed about his hitting. Perhaps Ichiro's unusual feelings were a product of Japanese culture. Remember that in high school, he was meant to feel shame for simply eating an ice cream cone. Or perhaps his father had made him feel that nothing was ever good enough—that he must get better and better and better.

More and more, Ichiro yearned to play in the major leagues. So many factors were in play: He long desired to test himself against the world's best players. Moving to a new country could be a way out of his unhappiness.

Ichiro's Japan Pacific League Statistics

Year	Age	Team	G	AB	R	H	2B	3B	HR	RBI	SB	CS	BB	SO	BA
1992	18	Orix	40	95	9	24	5	0	0	5	3	2	3	11	.253
1993	19	Orix	43	64	4	12	2	0	1	3	0	2	2	7	.188
1994	20	Orix	130	546	111	210	41	5	13	54	29	7	51	53	.385
1995	21	Orix	130	524	104	179	23	4	25	80	49	9	68	52	.342
1996	22	Orix	130	542	104	193	24	4	16	84	35	3	56	57	.356
1997	23	Orix	135	536	94	185	31	4	17	91	39	4	62	36	.345
1998	24	Orix	135	506	79	181	36	3	13	71	11	4	43	35	.358
1999	25	Orix	103	411	80	141	27	2	21	68	12	1	45	46	.343
2000	26	Orix	105	395	73	153	22	1	12	73	21	1	54	36	.387
Totals			951	3,619	658	1,278	211	23	118	529	199	33	384	333	.353

G = games AB = at-bats R = runs H = hits 2B = doubles 3B = triples HR = home runs RBI = runs batted in SB = stolen bases CS = caught stealing BB = walks SO = strikeouts BA = batting average

* Selected to AL All-Star team
Source: BaseballReference.com

Moreover, the BlueWave fell into mediocrity after their 1996 Japan Series win and attendance kept dropping. Also, Ichiro spent time in the United States and enjoyed it. In 1999, he attended spring training with the Seattle Mariners, who were partially owned by a Japanese businessman. It was there that Mariners superstar Ken Griffey Jr. looked at Ichiro's backside and said, "He's got no booty."[13] On December 3, 1999, Ichiro and Yumiko

In 2000, Ichiro gave a press conference to announce his next move. He would be leaving the Orix BlueWave and moving to America.

got married in the United States—in Santa Monica, California.

In 2000, Ichiro broke out of his hitting "slump," batting a Japan League-record .387 while playing 105 games. An injury ended his season and, as it turned out, his career in Japan.

Ichiro was headed to America.

Chapter 4

ICHIGAGA!

Beginning in the fall of 2000, Ichiro embarked on an extraordinary, almost unbelievable twelve-month period. He changed hemispheres, sparked mania in America, smashed records, won a dizzying number of games, staged a boycott, and experienced a national tragedy.

It all began when Ichiro's contract with the Orix BlueWave expired. Although he was technically free to play in the United States, the twenty-seven-year-old still had many hurdles to overcome before becoming a major-leaguer.

The main hurdle was his conscience. Loyalty is an important virtue in Japan, and Ichiro had to decide whether to abandon his country. At least one Japanese journalist had referred to pitcher Hideo Nomo's departure in 1995 as the "Shame of Japan."[1] Fortunately for Ichiro, Nomo's success in the United States sparked excitement back home. The Japanese seemed to delight in watching their countryman strike out major-leaguers. Even though Ichiro believed strongly in the principle of loyalty, his desire to play in America overpowered that feeling—and his countrymen did not seem to view his jump as shameful.

By the late 1990s, NPB and MLB worked out a complicated plan to allow Japanese players to compete in the majors. In summary, an MLB team would have to pay a large fee to NPB just for the right to negotiate with that player. Ichiro's American agent, Tony Attanasio, said that only MLB teams in cities with a strong Asian presence should bid on Ichiro. This meant West Coast teams.

The Seattle Mariners' large bid of $13.125 million earned them the chance to negotiate with Ichiro's agent—coupled with their strong Asian connections. In 2000, approximately one in six Seattle residents were of Asian descent. The Mariners also boasted a longtime NPB pitcher whom Ichiro knew and liked: Kazuhiro Sasaki, the 2000 AL Rookie of the Year. Ichiro, who previously had played with the Mariners during spring training, felt comfortable with the team.

While the $13.125 million went to the NPB, the Mariners had plenty of money left for Ichiro. In November 2000, they signed him to a three-year, $14 million contract. They also threw in English lessons and an interpreter for their new right fielder. Ichiro's mother worried about her son living in a foreign land, but she and Nobuyuki supported his decision. As for Ichiro himself, "I feel like a high school player a couple of days before the draft—very nervous, very excited, very eager to play in the US," he said.[2]

Madonna, Elvis . . . Ichiro

As spring training 2001 approached, "Ichiro Mania" began. Never before had such a huge Japanese star left for the majors. In addition, Ichiro—along with fellow Japanese hitter Tsuyoshi Shinjo at the same time—was the first Asian-born nonpitcher to compete in the major leagues.

Musaru Ikei, political science professor emeritus at Keio University, feared for the future of Japanese baseball. "Japanese teams will become the minor league teams of Major League ballclubs," Ikei worried. "If Ichiro succeeds, other fielders will follow one after the other . . . just like Russian ice hockey, which now has no power and no popularity" because their best players had signed with NHL teams.[3]

Others in Japan fretted that Ichiro would struggle in the majors due to his small size, thus making Japanese baseball seem inferior. "Japanese fans expect him to achieve the same thing he did in Japan, but it's too much," said Daisuke Araki, who had pitched in NPB and coached in the Cleveland Indians' minor league system. "I don't think Ichiro can beat the top-class US players, but he'll be able to play well with average Major League players."[4]

Ichiro tried on his Mariners jersey for the first time at a press conference. There was a lot riding on his move to the MLB.

When Ichiro arrived for spring training in Peoria, Arizona, he had the stage all to himself. After the 1999 season, Mariners superstar Ken Griffey Jr.—probably the greatest player on earth during the 1990s—left Seattle as a free agent. Following the 2000 season, superstar Alex Rodriguez fled the Mariners, too. He signed a free agent deal with the Texas Rangers for a record-setting $252 million, spread over ten years.

The American and Japanese press took a keen interest in Ichiro that spring. Americans were astounded to see up to a hundred Japanese reporters covering his spring training games. Ted Heid, a baseball scout who had been to Japan, explained: "He is Michael Jordan in Japan. Michael Jordan, Madonna, Elvis."[5] In fact, in a Japanese poll, Ichiro edged out his country's emperor as the most recognizable person in the country—a nation of 127 million people.

Wassup, Dawg?

While adjusting to a new team, new culture, and tremendous scrutiny, Ichiro batted .321 in spring training. Teammates marveled at his blazing speed, rocket arm, and flexibility during his stretches. Most of all, they were amazed at his ability to spray line drives all over the field. "It's like he's playing T-ball out there," said teammate Mike Cameron. "He hits wherever he wants to whenever he wants to."[6]

The Marines loved their new teammate, whom they called "Wizard." He greeted them with "Wassup?" and "Dawg," words he knew from the hip-hip music

Japanese Natives Who Starred in the Majors

Japanese-Born Players with 500 Hits in MLB

Player	Years	Hits	HRs	BA
Ichiro Suzuki	2001–2015	2,935	113	.314
Hideki Matsui	2003–2012	1,253	175	.282
Kazuo Matsui	2004–2010	615	32	.267
Nori Aoki	2012–2015	563	24	.287

Japanese-Born Starting Pitchers with 500 Strikeouts in MLB

Player	Years	SOs	Record	ERA
Hideo Nomo	1995–2008	1,918	123–109	4.24
Hiroki Kuroda	2008–2014	986	79–79	3.45
Daisuke Matsuzaka	2007–2014	720	56–43	4.45
Yu Darvish	2012–2015	680	39–25	3.27
Tomo Ohka	1999–2009	590	51–68	4.26
Hisashi Iwakuma	2012–2015	551	47–25	3.17

Japanese-Born Relief Pitchers with 50 Saves in MLB

Player	Years	Saves	Record	ERA
Kazuhiro Sasaki	2000–2003	129	7–16	3.14
Koji Uehara	2009–2015	86	17–19	2.42
Takashi Saito	2006–2012	84	21–15	2.34

All stats through 2015 season.

he listened to. They teased the rookie by replacing the clothes in his locker with a skirt and a woman's shirt. And teammate Bret Boone enjoyed the rice balls that Yumiko made. Sometimes, he and Ichiro would eat out of the same rice bowl.[7]

In Seattle, Mayor Paul Schell proclaimed April 1 "Ichiro Suzuki Day." The next day, hours before the season opener, Japanese American organizations held a ninety-minute ceremony for their new hero in Seattle. A somewhat embarrassed Ichiro attended, cheered on by more than two thousand fans.

That evening, Seattle hosted the Oakland Angels on Opening Night. In an ESPN.com poll of prominent baseball writers, all twelve picked Oakland to win the AL West Division that year. Six picked the Mariners to finish in second place, five in third place, and one in fourth (last) place.[8] The Mariners had gone 91–71 the previous year, but the loss of Rodriguez was supposed to be devastating. No way could Ichiro overcome the loss of A-Rod. Mariners manager Lou Piniella said he'd be happy if Ichiro hit just .270 or .280.

As it turned out, Ichiro would shine as the league MVP and the Mariners would record the most wins of any team in the 101-year history of the American League!

A Magical Start

Safeco Field, which had opened in 1999, offered a gorgeous view of downtown Seattle behind the left field seats. Because of all the rain Seattle experiences, the

Number 51 ran the bases on April 1, 2001, which was declared Ichiro Suzuki Day.

By the All-Star break, the Mariners stood at 63–24, with an enormous nineteen-game lead over second-place Oakland. In this fairytale season, Ichiro earned the most votes for the MLB All-Star Game—which was played in Seattle. He led off the first inning against Randy Johnson, who now wore number 51 for Arizona. The confrontation was almost comical. Johnson, the tallest player in MLB history at six feet ten inches (208 cm), towered over little Ichiro. The "Big Unit," who would strike out a record 419 batters in the regular season and postseason in 2001, tried to blow away his fellow 51 with a 100-mph (161-km) fastball. Ichiro ripped it for a single. He then stole second base as the crowd went wild. The AL prevailed over the NL 4–1, as Seattle pitcher Freddy Garcia earned the win and Kazuhiro Sasaki got the save.

Blazing to 200

For the Mariners, the 2001 season seemed like a Hollywood movie, filled with dramatic ups and downs. Ichiro, of course, was the main celebrity. He even battled the "paparazzi."

In Japan, the press was not allowed in the clubhouse, but that wasn't the case in the United States. Each game, large numbers of Japanese reporters and camera crews hounded Ichiro near his locker. Like a turtle, he retreated into a partial shell. He typically stared at his locker and responded to their questions with brief answers. He didn't mind the more professional reporters, but he knew that some were trying to make money off his fame. One Japanese magazine reportedly offered Ichiro $2 million to pose naked. He sarcastically said that he would do it if the people "who invade my privacy . . . would disappear from the planet."[12]

One day in mid-July, Ichiro couldn't leave his home because Japanese photographers were blocking his driveway. That was the final straw. For several games, he and his friend Sasaki boycotted the Japanese media. They refused to talk to them. For some reason, the boycott coincided with his worst hitting slump of the season.

Ichiro, who batted just .268 in July, heated up again in August. In twenty-eight games, he smashed 51 hits, stroking .429. Over one stretch, he hit safely in twenty-

The press had been barred from locker rooms in Japan, so Ichiro was uncomfortable with interview requests in the Mariners clubhouse. Eventually he learned to adjust, however.

one straight games. For the fourth (of five) time that year, he was named AL Rookie of the Month.

He perhaps should have been AL *Player* of the Month, but the honor went to Jermaine Dye of Oakland. The Angels were winning like crazy, going 64–18 over the final three months. Still, they couldn't come close to catching Seattle in the AL West. Consistently dominant, the Mariners' *worst* months of the season were June and July, when they went 18–9 and 18–9.

On August 28, Ichiro laced his 200th hit. Since 1935, no MLB player had reached 200 more quickly in a season. On September 10, he was batting .347 and the Mariners boasted a record of 104–40. And then . . . disaster struck.

The Tragedy of 9/11

On September 11, Islamic extremists hijacked jet airplanes and deliberately crashed two of them into the Twin Towers of the World Trade Center in New York City. Nearly three thousand people died. The terrorist group also flew another plane into the Pentagon in Washington, DC. It was the most deadly attack on American soil in history.

As rescue workers dug through the rubble in New York, searching for bodies of the living and dead, the nation mourned. All major league games were canceled for an entire week. The Mariners were in Anaheim, California, hoping to clinch the division title with wins over the Angels. But "in some ways, you don't even feel like playing anymore," said Mariners reliever Jeff Nelson. Added manager Piniella, "Your thoughts and your prayers are with these people. It's going to be very, very difficult when we start playing again."[13]

Yumiko was with Ichiro in Anaheim at the time. For them, as well as Sasaki, the 9/11 tragedy sparked memories of the devastating 1995 earthquake in Kobe. "This is a tragedy," Sasaki said. "I'm very saddened by it. Something like this should never happen."[14]

With American flags stitched on their uniforms, the Mariners' season renewed on September 18. The next day they clinched the AL West with a 5–0 win over Anaheim in Seattle. Instead of a wild celebration, the mood—due to the national tragedy—was happy but subdued. Players hugged each other on the field, with Piniella adding a few extra pats on the back for Ichiro.

A Season for the Ages

After losing the regular season finale on October 7, the Mariners looked back on their season with amazement. They had gone 116–46, setting the American League record for wins. Only the 1906 Chicago Cubs, who had gone 116–36 in the National League, had ever won that many games in a major league season. Bret Boone, formerly known as an average hitter, blasted .331 with 37 homers and a league-best 141 RBI. Yet not even he could match the performance of Ichiro.

Ichiro cracked 242 hits—an MLB rookie record, the ninth most in history at the time, and the most in the majors since 1930. Ichiro captured the AL batting title by hitting .350, and he led the league in steals with 56. He also scored 127 runs and belted 34 doubles, 8 triples, and 8 home runs. Defensively, he led all AL right fielders with 335 catches *and* made just one error all season. His tremendous range and rocket arm earned him an AL Gold Glove Award as one of the league's three best defensive outfielders.

Despite their season-long dominance, the Mariners fell behind Cleveland two games to one in the AL Division Series. But after losing Game 3 by the score of 17–2, the Mariners won the final two games to clinch. Ichiro sprayed 12 hits during the series and batted .600.

The AL Championship Series was a much different story. The New York Yankees had won three World Series in a row, and this year they had a new mission: Give their city something to feel good about. In late September, Yankee Stadium hosted a memorial service for the victims of the 9/11 attacks. Oprah Winfrey cohosted the event, and Bette Midler sang "Wind Beneath My Wings" while family members of victims and heroes cried in the stands. In the American League Championship Series (ALCS), emotions remained raw in New York.

In this series, Ichiro struggled at the plate, batting just .222. Though Seattle took Game 3 in New York, 14–3, the Yankees won the other four games. Their 12–3 rout in Game 5, also in New York, ended Seattle's season. Many Yankees fans chanted, "USA! USA!" Others were more mean-spirited, chanting "Ichiro, Sayonara! Ichiro, Sayonara!" In Japanese, *sayonara* means good-bye.

The drama of the 2001 season continued in the World Series between New York and the Arizona

Diamondbacks. Arizona won the first two games at home, but the momentum changed in Game 3 in New York. President George W. Bush threw the ceremonial first pitch and fired a strike, sparking bedlam among the patriotic crowd. Yankees Tino Martinez and Scott Brosius belted two-out, ninth-inning, game-tying home runs in Games 4 and 5, respectively, and the Series went to seven games. Arizona rallied with two runs in the bottom of the ninth of Game 7, ending the Yankees' dream.

Rookie MVP

In 2001 postseason award voting, some of the selections were no-brainers. St. Louis Cardinals slugger Albert Pujols was the unanimous winner of the NL Rookie of the Year Award after batting .329 with 37 homers and 130 RBIs. San Francisco Giants great Barry Bonds, who set a major league record with 72 home runs, breezed to the NL MVP Award. In the AL, twenty-seven out of twenty-eight voters chose Ichiro as the AL Rookie of the Year.

Those winners were all expected. But who would win the AL MVP Award? Some said it should be Bret Boone, while others supported Oakland basher Jason Giambi, who had belted .342 with 47 doubles and 38 homers. In the official balloting, Ichiro prevailed, earning 289 total votes compared to Giambi's 281. Voters felt that Ichiro's 242 hits and base stealing energized Seattle's offense and that his defense contributed to victories, too. He thus

Ichiro answered questions at a press conference at the Mariners clubhouse after he was named the American League's Most Valuable Player in 2001.

became just the second rookie (joining Boston's Fred Lynn in 1975) to win an AL or NL MVP Award.

As expected, Ichiro accepted the award with grace and humility. "I am honored just to be considered with all those great players," he said. As for his buddy Boone, he said, "I hope we can eat from the same rice bowl again [next season]."[15] Ichiro said he planned to celebrate the achievement with his wife Yumiko and a friend. It would be a quiet get-together . . . with no Japanese media allowed.

Incredibly, Ichiro's amazing 2001 story wasn't yet over. Many months earlier, former All-Star pitcher Rob Dibble had predicted that Ichiro would struggle in the major leagues. Dibble, a huge guy who overpowered hitters with 100-mph fastballs, had little faith in the small Japanese hitter. Dibble said if Ichiro batted .300 in 2001, he would run around New York City's Times Square wearing a tiny Speedo swimsuit. If Ichiro won the AL batting title, he'd prance around Times Square naked!

"Many of you may think I won't run," Dibble wrote on ESPN.com on October 4, 2001. "Trust me; I'm a man of my word. And my word is as good as Ichiro is a hitter."[16] On December 17, Dibble ran around Times Square wearing a Speedo. Yes, he had promised to take it all off for the batting title, but New York City police told him to keep it on.

And thus concluded the tale of Ichiro's extraordinary rookie season. In Seattle, fans couldn't wait for the spring of 2002.

Chapter 5

Hit Machine

In Japan in 2002, a Pepsi advertisement featured a picture of Ichiro swinging a bat next to the words "Change the World." This relentless hitter was doing just that. With his spectacular 2001 season, Ichiro had turned Japanese baseball on its head. Attendance for his former team, the Orix BlueWave, plummeted 17 percent in 2001. Where did the fans go? To their television sets. TV viewership of MLB games tripled in Japan that year.

Many Japanese even flew to Seattle to watch Ichiro play. Michael Kurtz, of the Seattle Convention and Visitors Bureau, noted that prior to 2001, about 105,000 to 110,000 Japanese citizens visited the state each year. For 2002, he predicted the number to surge to 150,000. "The Japanese like to go to famous places—the famous mountain is in Banff, Canada, the famous beach in Hawaii," said Don Lorentz, director of trade

Ichiro displays his Silver Slugger Award and his Gold Glove Award with Mariners team President Chuck Armstrong.

and development for the Port of Seattle. "We've always struggled to find that one thing. Now we have a great baseball player."[1]

Meanwhile, Japanese players started thinking about following Ichiro and Tsuyoshi Shinjo to the United States. Shinjo had batted just .249 during his NPB career, but he ripped .268 as a rookie with the New York Mets in 2001. If an ordinary hitter like Shinjo could excel in the United States, players thought, so can they.

"Now the doors are open," said Los Angeles Dodgers pitching coach Jim Colborn, "and everyone [in Japan] who has ever considered trying to play in the Majors is considering it even more strongly."[2]

In April 2002, four more Japanese players debuted in the major leagues: pitchers Kazuhisa Ishii, Takahito Nomura, and Satoru Komiyama and outfielder So Taguchi. However, these four players were mediocre at best in the majors. Even Shinjo tailed off in 2002, hitting just .238. The large wave of Japanese talent would never come; instead, just two to five players a year would trickle in.

Ichiro, apparently, was one of a kind.

Sophomore Slump or *SI* Jinx?

Ichiro got off to a quiet start in 2002, hitting .316 through April, but on May 2 he scored three runs on a magical night in Chicago. White Sox pitcher Jon Rauch opened the game by hitting Ichiro with a pitch. Bret Boone and Mike Cameron followed with back-to-back home runs—and later in the inning, they both reached the seats again!

Ichiro's Awards and Honors

Japan Pacific League
3-time League MVP, 1994–1996
7-time All-Star, 1994–2000
7-time batting champion, 1994–2000
5-time hits leader, 1994–1998
7-time Golden Glove Award winner, 1994–2000
League record for hits in a season, 210, 1994
League record for batting average in a season, .387, 2000
Japan Series champion, 1996

American League
Rookie of the Year, 2001
League MVP, 2001
10-time All-Star, 2001–2010
2-time batting champion, 2001, 2004
3-time Silver Slugger Award winner, 2001, 2007, 2009
10-time Gold Glove Award winner, 2001–2010
MLB record for hits in a season, 262, 2004
MLB record for 200-hit seasons, 10, 2001–2010

Following the 10-run inning, Cameron homered in the third and fifth innings. That made him the thirteenth player in MLB history to belt four longballs in a game, and he still had four innings to go. In his remaining two at-bats, Cameron was hit by a pitch and flew out to the warning track. With a little more oomph, he could have become the first player ever to belt five homers in a game. Seattle won, 15–4.

The next day, the Mariners visited Yankee Stadium, the site of their playoff exit in 2001. Ichiro ripped six hits in the three-game series (all Seattle victories) and began his own stretch of hot hitting. From May 3 to June 6, he drilled .441, upping his average to .384. Teammate Mark McLemore claimed that Ichiro was even better than in 2001 "because he knows the pitchers better, he knows how they're going to try to work him. He's taking more walks, too."[3]

Ichiro countered that "I don't think I'm better. It's been many years since I started playing. After playing so many years, it's hard to think of something drastically different from previous years. The numbers always change, day to day, but technique or skill, both of those elements probably stay the same and won't change drastically."[4]

By the All-Star break, the Mariners stood at 55–33. Ichiro, who once again led all All-Star Game vote-getters, entered the break with a .357 average. *Sports Illustrated* put his face on their cover that week next to the words "The Improbable Impact of Ichiro: 'I am very rare.'"

S. L. Price's article discussed one of Ichiro's pregame rituals. For twenty minutes, he wrote, Ichiro sat "on a chair in front of his locker: feet drawn up, heels pressed against his butt, knees together—a position physically impossible." Ichiro was watching a video of the pitcher he would face that night, "looking for weakness. No teammate speaks to him. His eyes shine. He looks hungry."[5]

Later in the season, however, Ichiro's hitting cooled off drastically. Perhaps, said the superstitious, it was the "sophomore slump." In sports, players who do well as a rookie often struggle in their second year. Ichiro said that even Japanese athletes talk about it. Perhaps the second-year player begins to doubt his abilities, or maybe opponents discover and exploit his weaknesses.

Others blamed Ichiro's slump on the "*Sports Illustrated* jinx." Ever since skier Jill Kinmont nearly died after appearing on *SI*'s cover in 1955, people have considered it a curse to be so featured. When reporters first told Ichiro about the curse in July 2002, he furrowed his brow and said, "Don't tell me that."[6] But something happened to his hitting. Ichiro batted .321 in July, .282 in August, and .248 in September.

Lou Piniella said that Ichiro may have been fatigued—that perhaps he had played his superstar too many games. A Yankees scout claimed that pitchers were throwing inside more on Ichiro, meaning he couldn't extend his arms and slap hits all over the field.[7] Still, he finished with a .321 average, 111 runs, 31 steals, and 208 hits, second most in the majors.

Though the Mariners finished with a splendid 93–69 record, they didn't make the playoffs. Oakland overtook first place in August while riding a twenty-game winning streak—with the last three wins coming in their final at-bat. This historic streak was featured in the popular book and film *Moneyball*. As for Ichiro, he and Yumiko packed their bags and returned to Japan for the off-season—an annual routine for them.

Like a Chef Treats His Knives

In 2002, Jim Caple of ESPN.com wrote a fascinating article on Ichiro's equipment. Just like his father had taught him during his childhood, Ichiro continue to oil his glove. His mitts were made annually by a Japanese man whom Ichiro knew personally. Ichiro treated his glove with great reverence, and he was appalled when he saw MLB players fling their mitts to the ground.

"Think about it," he said. "Those bats and gloves are not machine-made—they are hand-made. If someone who makes a glove or bat sees their product thrown away they will be very sad about it."[8]

Ichiro treated his bats with even more care. Produced by the Mizuno equipment company in Japan, each of his bats was jet black, measured 33.5 inches (85 cm), and weighed approximately 32 ounces (907 grams). His bats had been made of tamo wood when he played in Japan, but in the United States he decided to switch to ash wood because they responded better to the American climate.

Ichiro also kept his bats in a humidor, which the Mariners kept in a locked room in the clubhouse. The humidor kept the bats at a humidity level that Ichiro deemed best. The respectful batsman never tossed his bats or, like some frustrated hitters do, smashed them to pieces. He wiped his bats of dirt and grass stains, and he personally took them to the locker room after games.

"To become a better player, you have to take care of your equipment," Ichiro said through his translator. "The same thing applies to a chef [and his knives]. You're a professional. You earn money with a profession; therefore, you respect the tools you use to earn the money."[9]

Hitting Like Godzilla

Kevin Appier couldn't believe it. On June 17, 2003, the Anaheim Angels pitcher didn't give Ichiro anything good to hit, but the red-hot hitter teed off anyway. In the first inning, Appier fired high and inside and Ichiro socked the ball into Safeco Field's right field seats. In the third inning, he golfed a breaking ball near his ankles deep into the right field bleachers. When Appier painted the outside corner with a pitch, Ichiro went the other way, lining a single that hit third base. He finished 4-for-4. "I was a pitcher," Ichiro said after the game, referring to his amateur days. "And if I pitched to me now, I don't think I would get this guy out."[10]

From May 31 to July 18, 2003, Ichiro went on one of his patented hot streaks. Over the forty-one-game span, he cracked .402, raising his average to .352. Once again he started in the All-Star Game, and this time he had some familiar company in the AL outfield. Hideki Matsui, affectionately known as "Godzilla," had made the All-Star team as a Yankees rookie.

After belting 50 home runs for Yomiuri in Japan's Central League in 2002, Matsui followed Ichiro to the United States. To this day, he remains the second best

Ichiro treats his baseball equipment with respect. He even keeps his bats in a humidor!

Japanese hitter, and the only feared power hitter, to play in the majors. Matsui averaged .297, 23 homers, and 110 RBIs with New York from 2003 to 2005. In clinching Game 6 of the 2009 World Series, he drove in six runs in the Yankees' 7–3 win over Philadelphia and was named World Series MVP.

Ichiro flexed his own "Godzilla" muscle in 2003. He belted 13 home runs, including a dramatic blast in Kansas City on July 18. With two outs in the ninth and Seattle down, 3–2, Ichiro socked a game-winning grand slam to right-center field.

Unfortunately, Ichiro followed the same pattern as the previous year. He batted just .242 in August and .273 in September. It seemed that the rigors of the season were taking their toll. The MLB schedule included 162 games, twenty-seven more than in Japan. With Seattle tucked into the northwest corner of the United States, traveling was brutal. The Mariners had to log more air miles than any other team. Moreover, in all of his seasons with the Mariners, Ichiro virtually never had a day off. He often led the league in at-bats, and he was frequently on base—and stealing bases. It's no wonder he was pooped late in the season!

Under new manager Bob Melvin, the Mariners in 2003 again finished 93–69 and missed the playoffs, this time by two games. No one could fault the defense. Seattle set a major league record for fewest errors in a season with just 65. Ichiro, who made just two miscues, won his third straight Gold Glove Award. He finished

Before a 2003 game that saw their teams competing, Ichiro caught up with fellow countryman Hideki Matsui of the New York Yankees. Matsui came to Major League Baseball in 2003.

second in the AL in hits (212) and seventh in batting (.312) and runs (111). Notably, Ichiro led the league in singles—a feat he would accomplish ten consecutive seasons. It's clear proof that he ranks among the greatest contact/line drive hitters who ever lived.

On October 22, 2003, Ichiro turned thirty years old. As a rule of thumb in baseball, that's the age where players begin to decline. They lose quickness and speed, and the body starts to wear down. The Mariners, however, had complete faith in their right fielder. After the 2003 season, they signed him to a new contract: four years, $44 million. He would reward them with his best season yet.

Hits by the Bunches

In the spring of 2004, Robert Whiting—an American expert on Japanese baseball—spoke about his new book, *The Meaning of Ichiro*. In an interview with the *Seattle Times*, he focused on Nobuyuki, Ichiro's father. "The guy's a madman," Whiting said. "He would stand in the freezing winter and watch every practice, the only guy in the stands, taking notes, refusing to sit down because his son couldn't sit down, refusing to eat or drink because his son couldn't eat or drink."

As for Nobuyuki's famous son, "He's a very intelligent guy, very well-mannered, but he seems socially distant from people, and I think that's a result [of his childhood]," Whiting said. "On the other hand, he's one of the greatest baseball players in the world."[11]

By the end of April 2004, with Ichiro batting just .255, fans began to doubt his greatness. Over his last 949 at-bats dating back to August 17, 2002, he had batted .290. The next day, everything changed. Beginning May 1, Ichiro started rifling shots all over the yard and didn't let up—a ferocious display that resulted in an unprecedented 262 hits.

In the month of May, Ichiro cracked an even .400 while surpassing 2,000 career hits—in Japan's Pacific League and the major leagues. He stroked 50 hits during the month, making him the first player with two 50-hit months in his career since Pete Rose (the all-time MLB hits leader) in the 1970s. Incredibly, Ichiro would drill 50 hits in a month three more times in 2004 alone.

He cooled off in June, stroking just .274 for the month, as manager Bob Melvin batted him third in the lineup for a short period. Come July, he heated up again, lacing .432 for the month. His twenty-one-game hitting streak began on the Fourth of July and continued through July 29, the day he went 5-for-7 against Anaheim. Of course, he led off for the AL All-Star team—and jacked a double.

Though batting .346 through July, Ichiro couldn't enjoy his success. The Mariners were 39–64, as the pitching was atrocious, giving up eighteen runs in a single game on July 16. "I've never been on a last-place team," Ichiro said. Even through his interpreter, his discontent and sarcasm came through: "If you can find a player on this team who is not frustrated, I want to talk to him. I'd like to see how he does that."[12]

On a ninety-degree day in Baltimore, Seattle played the Orioles in a doubleheader. Ichiro went 5-for-5 with a triple in the opening game. Melvin kept him out of the lineup in the second game, but Ichiro came in late and smacked a single. Following that 6-for-6 day, he ripped six more hits over the next two games.

In Kansas City on August 18, rookie pitcher Jimmy Serrano hit him in the helmet with a pitch. Fans stared in stunned silence as Ichiro lay facedown in the dirt for several minutes. He eventually walked off the field. "I'm feeling dizzy," he said afterward. "I don't know if I'm going to be able to go tomorrow. I'm going to have to think about that tonight. That's why I'm not happy."

Ichiro took the next day off. Over the following two days, he went 7-for-10. His average stood at .366, and the press reported that he was on pace to tie George Sisler's MLB record for hits in a season. "I don't feel like I'm hot right now," he said at the time. "At this point in my career, I *should* be doing what I'm doing."[13]

For August, Ichiro bashed .463 with 56 hits—the most by a major-leaguer in a month since 1938. "Just watching that guy hit is amazing," marveled Seattle rookie Bobby Madritsch. "You could skip-bounce it into home plate, and he'll still hit a double. Guy's unbelievable."[14]

Those who predicted another September slump by Ichiro were greatly mistaken. He began the month batting .371 and finished it hitting .371. Highlights included 5-for-5 games against the Chicago White Sox and Anaheim. On October 1, he tied and broke Sisler's record.

On the year, Ichiro finished with 262 hits and won his second batting title (.372). Still lightning quick, he stole 36 bases and led the majors with 57 infield hits. "This is the most prolific hitter, leadoff guy, to play this game," Melvin said. "He is the best at what he does."[15]

A Small Dive in 2005

In 2005, the Mariners welcomed a teenage pitcher and a new manager. Felix Fernandez, a flame-throwing Venezuelan, would become the greatest pitcher in Mariners history. Fans would wear crowns to games to honor "King Felix," and those sitting in the "King's Court" would raise "K" cards, the symbol for strikeout.

But Fernandez wouldn't debut until August. In the meantime, Ichiro remained "king" in Seattle.

Mike Hargrove took over as Seattle's new manager. As an MLB hitter, he was known as the "Human Rain Delay" because of all the time he took between pitches. Prior to Ichiro's major league debut, Hargrove had predicted that the Japanese transfer would be nothing more than a "fourth outfielder" in the majors—not good enough to start. In 2005, he penciled Ichiro into the lineup in all 162 games.

Unfortunately in 2005, Ichiro suffered through his worst season in twelve years. He batted .243 in June and .244 in August, and he finished at .303. Still, he reached one thousand career MLB hits faster than any other player in history (696 games), and he topped two hundred hits for the fifth straight year. He also set career highs with 12 triples (which set a Mariners record) and 15 home runs.

Despite his enormous success, Ichiro remained surprisingly low profile. He didn't appear in advertisements because he didn't want to represent products that he wouldn't naturally support. His agent, Tony Attanasio, told the *Washington Post* that Ichiro turned down approximately $30 million a year in endorsement deals. The *Post* article noted that Ichiro liked glitzy things, such as "space-age, silver-trimmed sunglasses that are designed to hold downloaded songs and play them through tiny earpieces." However, the article added, he "shuns attention."[16] Ichiro performed many charitable acts, but he made sure to keep them private.

"Ichiro is a very nice man and a joy to be around," said Howard Lincoln, the Mariners' chief executive. "He's a genuinely warm individual." But, Lincoln said, it was important for Ichiro that "he has no distractions. He literally trains 365 days a year."[17]

"I Feel Ashamed"

Ichiro struggled with failure around this point of his career. The Mariners' subpar play (fewer than seventy wins again in 2005) troubled him, and he voiced his complaints to manager Hargrove after the season. In March, Ichiro represented Japan in the inaugural World Baseball Classic—a tournament that matches teams from sixteen countries. He batted just .231 as Japan was eliminated after two games. "I feel ashamed," he said afterward. "If I were satisfied with my performance, I should quit baseball."[18]

Ichiro wasn't too pleased either when he opened the MLB season batting .177 over his first fifteen games. Not surprisingly, he eventually caught fire, batting .474 over a twenty-two-game stretch. In early June, he won the AL Player of the Week Award, then surprised reporters with his unusual reaction. "I didn't know there was such an award," he said, even though he had earned the honor previously. The award came with a gift—a new watch. "I collect watches," Ichiro said. "The watch I'll get probably won't be in my taste." What kind of watches did he collect? "That's personal," he said.[19]

Ichiro is known almost as much for his bold fashion sense as he is for racking up the hits.

On the season, he rapped .322 and stroked 224 hits, tops in the majors. Instead of losing speed at age thirty-two, Ichiro stole 45 bases in 47 attempts. From April 29 to season's end, he stole 39 bags without being caught—a single-season American League record.

Nevertheless, the Mariners finished below .500 again at 78–84, much to Ichiro's displeasure. The next season would be the last on his contract. Rumors flew that it would be his final year in Seattle. He was tired of losing.

But a funny thing happened in 2007. The Mariners started winning again, thanks largely to another amazing season by number 51.

Chapter 6

Battles in Seattle

During the 2006 to 2007 off-season, while home in Japan, Ichiro criticized his Seattle teammates. He told a reporter that they weren't as committed to winning as they should be. He didn't like how they played cards in the clubhouse while the team was struggling. When he arrived at spring training in 2007, he informed the press that he might leave the Mariners after his contract expired in October. He wanted to play for a winner.

It appeared that the "love affair" between Seattle fans and Ichiro was coming to an end. In May, in a rare in-depth interview, he explained that he had put the "Ichigaga" mania behind him. "Many people have this image of me," he told *USA Today*,

> For a long time, I cared about that. I often thought about what I could do to please them. I was always chasing after that Ichiro. It became a struggle. I think I was scared of what people were thinking of me.
>
> After 2004, I realized it was impossible to please them. I discovered I needed to do what I needed to, [and] if people like it, that's good. I became more confident. And that Ichiro became a part of me instead of me chasing after him.
>
> When people get placed upon a pedestal—when they start chasing after that person on the pedestal—they become mannequin-like. People striving for approval from others become phony. You should seek approval from yourself.[1]

The "new," more mature Ichiro continued to shine on the diamond in 2007—and his team began to win. With a walk-off victory on July 1—their eighth triumph in a row—the Mariners boasted a 45–33 record. Powerful third baseman Adrian Beltre and right fielder Carlos Guillen provided offensive firepower. Ichiro, playing center field regularly for the only season of his career, sparked the offense with his leadoff skills. He extended his streak of stolen bases without being caught to 45, an AL record. He went 5-for-5 on May 15 during a twenty-five-game hitting streak, which set a Mariners record. In the All-Star Game, he continued to make history.

All-Star Artist

Ichiro entered the All-Star break batting .359, and he continued to smoke the ball in the All-Star Game in San Francisco. FOX announcer Joe Buck described his blast in the fifth inning at AT&T Park: "Here's a shot into deep right field—back at the wall. Ichiro hits it *off* the wall. It takes a weird carom, and Ichiro *may* circle the bases! In to score is Roberts. Here comes Ichiro! Inside-the-park home run!"[2]

Ichiro had initially thought the ball was going to clear the brick wall. "When it didn't, I was really bummed," he said. Instead, he tallied the first inside-the-park homer in All-Star Game history.[3] He went 3-for-3 on the night and earned the game's MVP Award. "He's an artist with that bat," NL manager Tony La Russa said afterward.[4]

Three days after the All-Star Game, with the Mariners at 50–36, the team announced it had signed Ichiro to

At the 2007 All-Star Game, Ichiro hit an inside-the-park home run against the National League. Despite being named game MVP, he was disappointed the ball didn't clear the wall.

a five-year contraction extension. From 2008 through 2012, Seattle would pay him $90 million. According to Ichiro, his dog Ikky had made the decision. Ikky said, "Ruff, ruff, ruff," Ichiro, smiling, said through an interpreter. "That means, 'Stay, stay, stay.'"[5]

Instead of the ups and downs of recent seasons, Ichiro maintained an average around .350 for the rest of the year. He finished at .351, second in the AL to Magglio Ordonez's .363, and cranked out an MLB-high 238 hits. Since 1930, the most major league hits in a season have been as follows: (1) Suzuki, 262 (2004); (2) Suzuki, 242 (2001); (3) Wade Boggs, 240 (1985); (4) Darin Erstad, 240 (2000); (5) Rod Carew, 239 (1977); (6) Don Mattingly, 238 (1986); and (7) Suzuki, 238 (2007).

In the end, Ichiro would have traded some of those hits for a few team victories. The Mariners finished 2007 with eighty-eight wins and missed the playoffs by six games.

Not Cool, Ichiro

Apparently, Ikky couldn't predict the future. If Ichiro or his pooch knew how lousy the 2008 season would be, he might not have re-signed with the team. The Mariners finished at 61–101. Felix Hernandez, at 9–11, was the only pitcher to win more than six games. General manager Bill Bavasi was fired in midseason. So too was manager John McLaren, replaced by Jim Riggleman.

Ichiro batted just .310 on the year. However, he did top one hundred runs for the eighth straight MLB season, and his 213 hits tied for the league lead. He stole

43 bases in 47 tries and earned his eighth straight All-Star trip and eighth consecutive Gold Glove Award. He also surpassed three thousand combined hits in Japan's Pacific League and the major leagues.

The losing season seemed to sour Ichiro's attitude. Rumors circulated that he did not get along with some of his teammates. In early May, with the Mariners in the midst of a losing streak and his batting average around .280, Ichiro visited Olympic View Elementary School. He and four teammates were supposed to speak to 350 students about D.R.E.A.M.: avoiding Drugs, learning Respect, valuing Education, having a good Attitude, and staying Motivated. Ichiro, through his interpreter, was scheduled to talk about "staying Motivated." Instead, he didn't say a word. The students, who had screamed Ichiro's name in their excitement, were disappointed. He left the event with just a wave. It was not like his first school visit in 2001, when he had sat on the floor and joked around with the kids.

Asked why Ichiro had clammed up, manager McLaren said, "Maybe he had a cold or something. I don't know."[6]

It was a bad day for Ichiro, worse than any 0-for-5 performance.

Despite his reserved personality, Ichiro still dazzled onlookers with his outfits. The *Toronto Star* caught him wearing "a green and white 1970s-style cap with the word 'Orange' on it—turned backward . . . His jeans were chic and faded, his footwear designer white sneakers."[7] The *McClatchy-Tribune Business News* described his

Ichiro charmed the elementary school students he spent time with as part of a Mariners outreach program. However, on one visit, he disappointed the excited students.

"backward trucker hat, designer polo shirt, custom Levi's that he helped design and Belgian paint-stained designer canvas sneakers."[8] Wow.

"It's something I really enjoy doing," he explained, "going to stores and seeing what looks good. All my teammates don't think what I'm wearing is good fashion. A lot of times they can't believe what I'm wearing."[9]

What's Up, Mr. President?

In 2009, the Mariners welcomed a new manager, Don Wakamatsu, who is half Japanese. During World War II, Wakamatsu's father was born in a Japanese internment camp in California. While the Mariners experienced an uneventful season in 2009 (85–77), Ichiro's year was quite remarkable. Off to a poor start in the World Baseball Classic in March, he began to feel the stress. Japan won the tournament and Ichiro knocked in the winning hit, but he suffered from bleeding gastric ulcers. He couldn't open the season for Seattle, and the Mariners put him on the disabled list for the first time in his MLB career.

The drama continued in his first game back, when he belted a grand slam against the Angels. From May 6 to June 3, Ichiro authored a twenty-seven-game hitting streak in which he batted .398. Up through July 17, he hit safely in sixty of sixty-three games. No one had done that since Joe DiMaggio in 1941, the year of his all-time record fifty-six-game hitting streak. He recorded the first walk-off hit of his major league career on July 28 against Toronto, then cracked another on September 14 versus the White Sox. The next day, he blasted a walk-off home run against Yankees legend Mariano Rivera before being mobbed at home plate.

Ichiro started in the All-Star Game in St. Louis, where he met President Barack Obama. While visiting both the NL and AL clubhouses, the nation's first African-American president met history's greatest Asian baseball player. Obama signed a ball for Ichiro, who bowed respectfully. "My idea, when I saw him, was to say, 'What's up?' to him," Ichiro said. "But I got nervous. You know, he has that kind of aura about him. So I got nervous and I didn't say that to him. I was a little disappointed about that. But I realized after seeing him today that presidents wear jeans, too. So my hope is that our skipper, Wakamatsu, was watching that and we can wear jeans on our flights, as well."[10]

On September 6, Ichiro stroked his 2,000th major league hit. Only Al Simmons had reached that milestone faster than Ichiro's 1,402nd game. Ken Griffey Jr. returned to the Mariners in 2009, and on September 13 he helped Ichiro celebrate a historic achievement. By beating out a slow grounder at Texas, Ichiro recorded his 200th hit of the year. It was his ninth consecutive 200-hit season, which broke Wee Willie Keeler's MLB record. From 1894 to 1901, the five-foot four-inch (163-cm) Keeler had slapped singles all over the field. "Hit 'em where

Ichiro had the honor of speaking personally with President Barack Obama in the locker room before the start of the MLB All-Star Game on July 14, 2009.

they ain't" was his motto. Ichiro was a similar player and, like Wee Willie, a little guy. Griffey celebrated by slinging Ichiro onto his shoulders and carrying him into the shower, then wrote silly things on the two hundred-hit ball. Meanwhile, the record-breaker's teammates showered him with beer.[11]

Otherwise, Ichiro couldn't really enjoy his achievement. "When I break a record, I never feel satisfaction," he said. "I strongly feel expectation from Japan and my records are things that I feel Japan [believes] they must have. I always want to feel satisfaction, but when I accomplish a record, I only feel relief."[12]

Ichiro finished 2009 with a .352 average (second in the AL) and a league-best 225 hits. It was his fifth season with at least 220 hits, a major league record. Unfortunately, he finished under one hundred runs (eighty-eight) for the first time in the majors, and he would never reach triple digits again. Ichiro, who turned thirty-six in October 2009, would soon show signs of wearing down.

10, 10, and 10 in 2010

The Mariners entered 2010 with high expectations. They were a team built on strong pitching and defense, but unfortunately they couldn't hit. As a team, they batted a stunningly low .236 and finished at 61–101. As usual, No. 51 despised all the losing. "To be honest with you, I can't even explain in words," he said in mid-July. "It's very, very tough, hard, and depressing."[13]

Ichiro batted .315 and stole 42 bases. But with no big sluggers in the lineup, he scored a mere 74 runs.

He did reach 200 hits yet again (league-best 214), tying Pete Rose's major record for the most 200-hit seasons in a career (10). Incredibly, he had accomplished the feat in just his tenth season! Ichiro also won his tenth Gold Glove Award, becoming the sixteenth player and sixth outfielder to achieve that feat. To this day, Al Kaline, Griffey, and Ichiro hold the AL record for most consecutive Gold Glove Awards. In addition, Ichiro made the AL All-Star team for the tenth and final time.

Despite Seattle's losing ways, Ichiro still flashed his competitive fire. Always hustling, he went 736 at-bats without hitting into a double play—the most by an MLB player since 1998. On August 4, the aging star stole four bases in one game against Texas. And on June 2, he starred in the "win one for Junior" game. Griffey had announced his retirement hours earlier, and the Mariners vowed to honor him with a win that night against Minnesota. With the game tied, 1–1, in the tenth inning, Ichiro fouled off seven pitches and then singled in the winning run.

"He's a superstar, and not just because of his numbers and his stats, but because of his personality," Ichiro said of Griffey that day. "He was about caring for each other. It's something we all need to learn from him, and it's what makes him better than a superstar."[14]

Honoring Those He Conquers

On April 2, 2011, Ichiro broke the record of another Mariners great. In his eighteen seasons, all with Seattle, Edgar Martinez had batted .312 and ripped 2,247 hits.

The seven-time All-Star was so revered that Major League Baseball named an annual award after him: the Edgar Martinez Outstanding Designated Hitter Award. That night, Ichiro beat out a single for his 2,248th career hit with Seattle, breaking Martinez's team record.

As he had with Griffey, Ichiro lavished praise on the man he surpassed. "I broke his record," Ichiro said after the game. "When you look at the numbers that's a fact. But he's a hero back in Seattle. He's my hero as well. When you look at his existence, he's a lot bigger than I am—being a great human being as well. So, that's how I look at it."[15]

Praising those he conquered became a running theme in Ichiro's life. He visited Wee Willie Keeler's grave and, in 2009, did the same for George Sisler. While in St. Louis for the All-Star Game that summer, Ichiro, Yumiko, and friends laid flowers at Sisler's grave at Des Peres Presbyterian Church Cemetery. It had been nearly five years since Ichiro had broken Sisler's season hits record. "I wanted to do that for a grand upperclassman of the baseball world," Ichiro said. "I think it's only natural for someone to want to do that, to express my feelings in that way."[16]

Ichiro expressed his reverence for the game's history by visiting the Baseball Hall of Fame and Museum in Cooperstown, New York—not once, but many times. Ichiro and Yumiko would spend hours touring the halls and admiring the exhibits.

In 2011, at age thirty-seven, Ichiro finally fell into decline. Though he stole 40 bases, he batted just .272. In the outfield, he didn't break quickly after fly balls like he had in the past. His streaks of ten straight 200-hit seasons, ten consecutive Gold Glove Awards, and ten straight All-Star team selections all came to an end. To cap it off, the Mariners finished in last place in the AL West with ninety-five losses.

No longer Superman, Ichiro was now Clark Kent, wrote Jerry Brewer of the *Vancouver Sun*. Ichiro, Brewer stated, was now "normal. There's no mystique about average performance. He's a 37-year-old man with salt invading the pepper in his hair . . . Well, at least he's still in great physical condition. If not, he probably would be done."[17]

"Overcome With Sadness"

In 2012, a new Japanese sensation arrived in the United States. Yu Darvish, a fireballer with a six-pitch repertoire, debuted with the Rangers that spring. Born in Japan to an Iranian father and Japanese mother, Darvish stood six feet five inches (196 cm). As an MLB rookie in 2012, he made the AL All-Star team and finished 16–9.

Meanwhile, fans in Japan still hailed Ichiro as a hero. When the Mariners visited the Tokyo Dome for an exhibition series in March, flashbulbs lit up the stadium whenever Ichiro stepped to the plate. Once the 2012 regular season began, it was back to reality. On June 19, the day of his 2,500th major league hit, Ichiro was batting just .265 and the Mariners were 30–40. Around

Chapter 7

4,000 AND BEYOND

For the 8,484th time, Ichiro strode to the batter's box in a regular-season major league game. The setting was familiar—Safeco Field—but everything else had changed. On this day, July 23, 2012, he wore a gray and black Yankees road uniform. He donned a new number, and he batted in an unfamiliar spot in the batting order.

"Batting eighth," boomed the public address announcer, "the right fielder, number 31, Ichiro Suzuki!"[1]

The Seattle crowd, thirty thousand strong, rose to its feet and applauded as one. Ichiro took some practice cuts and then, before stepping into the box, turned to the fans on the first base side. He took off his helmet and bowed deeply to them. He turned to the other side and bowed again. The gesture of respect swelled the applause. In the stands, a fan raised a poster that said "Sayonara Suzuki."

Just after being traded, Ichiro acknowledged fans at Safeco Field in Seattle in his first at-bat as a Yankee.

Next to those words was a sad face, with a tear falling. Throughout Safeco, fans brushed away real tears as well.

On the second pitch, Ichiro ripped a line drive up the middle. Same swing, different team.[2]

After a decade of losing, Ichiro expressed his excitement for playing with the Yankees. Baseball's winningest team ever (twenty-seven World Series titles), New York stood in first place in the AL East Division at the time of the trade. The "Bronx Bombers" boasted a lineup full of superstars: Derek Jeter, Robinson Cano, Mark Teixeira, Curtis Granderson, and two former Mariners: Alex Rodriguez and Raul Ibanez. Manager Joe Girardi batted Ichiro eighth to generate more offense at the bottom of the order.

Media swarmed Ichiro in New York, but he was used to that. In fact, several Japanese sportswriters moved to New York and continued to cover him—like they had for twelve years in Seattle. Ichiro, who had long despised the throng of Japanese reporters, mellowed in his later years.

"Having them here really helps out," Ichiro said. "I've spent a lot of time with them and built a business relationship, and it's taken a long time to have that relationship. If they weren't here, I'd have to start from scratch, and trust somebody, and build that relationship again."[3]

Yankees' Hottest Hitter

Ichiro found new life with the contending Yankees in 2012. In sixty-seven games with New York, he cracked

.322—the highest average on the club—and stole 14 bases. He moved up in the order, and his .385 average in September helped the Yankees edge the Baltimore Orioles by two games in the AL East. The Yankees then played Baltimore in the AL Division Series and beat them, 3–2. In the sixth inning of Game 5, Ichiro doubled in Jeter to give New York a 2–0 lead. They won, 3–1.

Disaster befell the Yankees in the AL Championship Series against Detroit. Jeter, the team captain and perhaps the biggest star in baseball, broke his ankle in Game 1. Cano and Granderson batted a combined 1-for-29 in the series, and A-Rod was hitting so badly that Girardi benched him—causing a huge controversy. In the Tigers' four-game sweep, Ichiro batted .353 and his teammates hit .130.

Ichiro batted just .262 with 20 steals for the Yankees in 2013. It was the worst season of his career, but not bad for a guy who would turn forty that October. Most notably, on August 21, he cracked his 4,000th career hit in Japan's and America's major leagues. In MLB history, only two men had reached 4,000—Pete Rose (4,256) and Ty Cobb (4,191).

Some wondered how people would react to Ichiro reaching that milestone. After all, it's the combination of two totals from two countries. Moreover some consider Japanese baseball to be slightly inferior to American baseball. When Ichiro stroked the 4,000th hit—an opposite-field single at Yankee Stadium against Toronto knuckleball pitcher R. A. Dickey—he reached first base

Ichiro's Secret Gym

In March 2013, Brad Lefton of the *Wall Street Journal* informed readers of the "Secret Gym of Ichiro Suzuki." During the off-season in Kobe, Japan, Ichiro worked out up to three times a day in his personal weight room. The gym included seven specially designed machines that not only strengthened muscles but improved flexibility.

With regular weight training machines, Ichiro explained, "you're fatigued at the end. But these have a completely opposite, invigorating effect because the movements they require help oxygenate the blood and optimize circulation."[4]

Ichiro worked on similar machines in his personal gyms in the United States. He believed that they helped keep his muscles healthy and strong. Never in his career had he landed on the disabled list due to a muscle-related injury.

and remained solemn faced. However, the fans rose to their feet and his Yankees teammates streamed out of the dugout.

Clapping along with the fans, the Yankees walked to Ichiro, patted his back, and gave him congratulatory hugs. Ichiro's stoic expression melted away, and he beamed a big, bright, giddy smile. After his teammates returned to the dugout, Ichiro doffed his helmet and bowed to the fans. They responded with a roar. It was another emotional, unforgettable moment in Ichiro's unique career.

"It was supposed to be a night that was special to me," Ichiro said after the Yankees' 4–2 win. "But . . . I wasn't expecting when my teammates came out to first base—that was very special. To see the fans, I wasn't expecting so much joy and happiness from them. That's what made it very special tonight. Not just the number, but all the things that happened with it."[5]

So Long, New York

The Yankees endured a disappointing 85–77 season in 2013, and a year later they won one fewer game. In neither year did they come close to the playoffs. In 2014, the Yankees featured three all-time greats: Ichiro (age

Ichiro celebrates his 4,000th career hit with his new teammates at Yankee Stadium on August 21, 2013. The reaction from fans and his teammates surprised and touched him.

forty), Derek Jeter (forty), and Alex Rodriguez (thirty-nine). It was Jeter's farewell season, and opposing teams honored him with ceremonies and gifts all season long. In his final home game, he drilled the game-winning hit, sparking near hysteria at Yankee Stadium. On the other end of the spectrum, A-Rod was suspended for the entire season for using performance-enhancing drugs. Ichiro's season fell in the middle; he batted .284—almost all singles.

Joel Sherman of the *New York Post* wrote that "Ichiro has seemed to enjoy his time in New York, finding comfort and camaraderie by having so many veterans of accomplishment around him."[6] However, his contract with New York expired after the 2014 season, and the Yankees had no desire to re-sign him. Ichiro insisted that he did not want to retire, and in January 2015 he signed as a free agent with the Miami Marlins.

Ichiro still loved the game, still dreamed of playing in a World Series, and was only 156 hits shy of three thousand in the major leagues. Only twenty-nine MLB players had reached 3,000 hits, and none had done it after winning seven batting titles in Japan! The Marlins foresaw him as a fourth outfielder and a strong, veteran leader in the clubhouse. They signed him to a one-year contract worth around $2 million. A few months earlier, the Marlins had signed their All-Star outfielder, Giancarlo Stanton, to a thirteen-year, $325 million contract—the richest in baseball history.

Now Pitching . . . Ichiro!

Many people move to Florida to retire, but Ichiro didn't think of himself as a senior citizen. "Hopefully it won't look like I'm using a bat as a cane," he joked to reporters in February 2015. "Everybody is treating me like I'm really old, but please, put me in that group of young guys. I feel young and want to be included in that group." He added that three thousand hits "is a goal of mine," but "what I wanted most was just the warm feelings the Marlins gave me."[7]

On the year, Ichiro garnered 398 at-bats and batted just .229. While teammate Dee Gordon won the batting title at .333, Ichiro had the sixth lowest average in the

After his contract with the Yankees expired, Ichiro signed with the Miami Marlins. Although he had accomplished so much in his career, he looked forward to meeting more of his goals.

league among those with at least 375 at-bats. He also remained sixty-five hits short of three thousand, and his team finished at 71–91. Yet Ichiro, who had often been upset early in his career when he failed to meet his high expectations, learned to enjoy the simple joys of the game.

Such was the case on April 29 against the New York Mets. Miami led, 4–3, in the bottom of the eighth, and Ichiro batted with two men on. He battled Alex Torres for eight pitches while the home crowd chanted his name. He then socked the ninth pitch into the seats. "I heard [the fans] during the at-bat," Ichiro said. "When I hit the home run, just to see my teammates so happy and the fans so happy, I was very moved and I almost cried . . . Special moments in a career I don't think are created by the player; they're created by others. That's what happened tonight."[8]

On the last day of the 2015 season, Ichiro got a chance to fulfill a lifelong dream—to pitch in the major leagues. With the Marlins trailing Philadelphia, 6–2, manager Dan Jennings instructed his forty-one-year-old outfielder to take the mound. With a big leg kick, Ichiro pitched a full inning, showing off his 87-mph (141-km) fastball, curveball, and change-up. He allowed two doubles and a run, but he retired the other three batters on two fly balls and a groundout. Smiling teammates greeted him in the dugout.

"The final day of the season, [players] earned the right to see a guy like Ichiro, a Hall of Famer, go out and

On October 4, 2015, Ichiro pitched for the Marlins against the Philadelphia Phillies.

throw that last inning and kind of punctuate his career," Jennings said.[9]

However, Ichiro's career was not yet over. Two days after the season, he signed a one-year contract. He would enter 2016 just forty-three hits shy of Pete Rose's total of 4,256.

Bound for Cooperstown

A hundred years from now, when a book is published on the history of baseball, Ichiro will be—or should be—featured prominently in the text. The book would note that he won seven consecutive batting titles in Japan, then became the first major-leaguer with ten consecutive 200-hit seasons. That's seventeen straight extraordinary seasons. Had he joined the Mariners in 1995 instead of 2001, he very well could have strung together sixteen consecutive 200-hit years in the majors. Remember, the previous record was eight straight, set by Wee Willie Keeler in the 1800s.

More importantly, wrote baseball historian Stuart Shea, Ichiro "forever destroyed the silly notion that Japanese players couldn't succeed in the Major Leagues."[10]

Fellow historian Gary Gillette expounded on the topic. "Just as there are few ballplayers known universally by their first name, there are also few ballplayers who can truly be said to have changed the game," Gillette wrote. "Ichiro's memorable debut season with Seattle in 2001 forever changed the patronizing perceptions of Japanese players in the United States. He is a true Hall of Famer,

Baseball fans won't likely forget Ichiro Suzuki, even after he retires. His place in the record books is assured for years to come!

and he paved the way for Asian players to become an integral part of 21st century Major League Baseball."[11]

Baseball historian Mark Armour offered this perspective:

> When Ichiro burst on the scene, we Americans had firmly settled on the most effective way to play baseball: become big as a house and hit the ball as far as you can. Ichiro landed as if on spaceship from an earlier age, with all his funky mannerisms, line drives, bullet pegs from right field, running first to third. He has a resume filled with awards, and All-Star Games, and records, plenty enough to keep him remembered forever. But more than that, Ichiro reminded us—and I do believe we needed reminding—how beautiful this game could be in the hands of an artist.[12]

No one doubts that Ichiro will be inducted into the Baseball Hall of Fame in Cooperstown. When that day comes, he will deliver a speech. He likely will mention his father, Nobuyuki, who practiced with him day after day, through the scorching heat of summer and the brutal chill of winter. During his speech, Ichiro likely will get emotional.

And once again, tears will flow.

Chronology

1973—Ichiro is born in Nichi Kasugai-gun, Aichi, Japan, on October 22.

1981—Begins to train daily with his father.

1991—Drafted by the Orix BlueWave in the fourth round of Japan's professional baseball draft.

1994—Wins the Pacific League batting title (.385) and becomes the first player in NPB history to reach two hundred hits in a season (210). Named league MVP.

1995—Repeats as Pacific League batting champion (.342), belts 25 homers, and earns the MVP Award.

1996—Again captures the batting title (.356) and MVP Award, and leads Orix to victory in the Japan Series.

1997—Wins the batting crown (.345) and drives in 91 runs.

1998—Leads Pacific League in hitting at .358.

1999—Wins his sixth bat title (.343) and doesn't make an error all year.

—Marries Japanese reporter Yumiko Fukushima on December 3.

2000—Sets Pacific League record with season average of .387.

—His contract is purchased by the Seattle Mariners on November 30.

2001—Goes 3-for-5 in his MLB debut on April 2.

—Voted to the All-Star Game with a record 3,373,035 votes in July.

—Leads AL in batting (.350), hits (242), and stolen bases (56).

—Named AL Rookie of the Year and AL MVP in November.

2002—Cracks 208 hits and bats .321.

2003—Raps .312 with 212 hits.

2004—Drills his 257th hit of the season to break George Sisler's MLB record on October 1.

—Finishes with 262 hits and wins the AL batting title (.372).

2005—Bats .303 and tallies 206 hits.

2006—Sets a single-season AL record with 39 consecutive successful stolen bases.

—Raps .322 with AL-best 224 hits.

2007—Legs out an inside-the-park home run in the MLB All-Star Game on July 10. Named game's MVP.

—Strokes .351 with league-high 238 hits.

2008—Tops AL again in hits (213) and bats .310.

2009—Meets President Obama at the All-Star Game on July 14.

—Knocks his 2,000th major league hit on September 6.

—Sets MLB record with his ninth straight 200-hit season on September 13.

—Enjoys his last great season, hitting .352 with a league-high 225 hits.

2010—Plays in his 10th straight, and final, All-Star Game on July 13.

—Ties Pete Rose's MLB record with his tenth 200-hit season on September 23.

—Cracks .315 with AL-best 214 hits.

—Wins tenth straight, and final, Gold Glove Award in November.

2012—Traded by Seattle to the New York Yankees on July 23.

—Bats .322 in regular season action for the Yankees.

—Rips .353 in New York's ALCS loss to Detroit in October.

2013—Records his 4,000th career hit (NPB and MLB combined) on August 21.

2015—Signs as a free agent with the Miami Marlins on January 27.

—Pitches an inning for the Marlins, allowing one run on October 4.

Chapter Notes

Chapter 1. All Hail Ichiro

1. "Ichiro Breaks the Single Season Hits Record," YouTube video, posted by richtrue, Mar. 22, 2010, https://www.youtube.com/watch?v=Tdf8mhUlz5c.
2. Ibid.
3. Ibid.
4. Ibid.
5. Associated Press, "Ichiro Passes Sisler, Pads Record." *ESPN.com,* Oct. 2, 2004, http://sports.espn.go.com/mlb/news/story?id=1893214 (accessed Nov. 2, 2015).
6. Ibid.
7. Ibid.
8. Ibid.
9. Ibid.
10. Jerry Brewer, "Superhero Ichiro Showing His Mortality," *Vancouver Sun*, July 8, 2011, ProQuest.

Chapter 2. A Million Swings

1. Robert Whiting, *The Meaning of Ichiro: The New Wave from Japan and the Transformation of Our National Pastime* (New York: Hachette, 2004). E-book.
2. Ibid.
3. Rob Rains, *Baseball Samurais: Ichiro Suzuki and the Asian Invasion* (New York: St. Martin's, 2001), p. 97.
4. Whiting.
5. Narumi Komatsu, *Ichiro on Ichiro* (Seattle: Sasquatch Books, 2004), p. 157.
6. Rains, p. 96.
7. Komatsu, p. 158.
8. Ibid.

9. Judith Levin, *Ichiro Suzuki* (New York: Chelsea House, 2007), p. 17.

CHAPTER 3. THE "MAN" IN JAPAN

1. Narumi Komatsu, *Ichiro on Ichiro* (Seattle: Sasquatch Books, 2004), p. 161.
2. Ibid., p. 163.
3. T. R. Reid, "Swinging a Mean Shovel," *Washington Post*, Oct. 12, 1994, ProQuest.
4. "Big-league Prospects," *Globe and Mail*, June 21, 1996, ProQuest.
5. "Ichiro Suzuki Pitching in Japanese All-Star Game 1996," posted by International Baseball, Mar. 12, 2009, https://www.youtube.com/watch?v=tvp-kuAX5Bg.
6. Komatsu, p. 86.
7. Judith Levin, *Ichiro Suzuki* (New York: Chelsea House, 2007), p. 41.
8. Michael Farber, "Rising Son," *SI.com,* Dec. 4, 2000, http://www.si.com/vault/2000/12/04/293082/rising-son-the-defection-of-ichiro-suzuki-a-career-353-hitter-isnt-seen-as-all-bad-news-in-japan-if-he-becomes-a-sensation-with-the-mariners-and-brings-honor-to-his-country (accessed Nov. 10, 2015).
9. David S. Leigh, *Ichiro Suzuki* (Minneapolis: Lerner Publishing Group, 2004), p. 53.
10. Ibid., p. 54.
11. Ibid., p. 60.
12. Komatsu, p. 92.
13. Mark Bechtel, "Rising Sons," *SI.com,* Apr. 23, 2001, http://www.si.com/vault/2001/04/23/301986/rising-sons-with-timely-hitting-and-superb-defense-the-mariners-ichiro-suzuki-and-the-mets-tsuyoshi

-shinjo-are-boosting-the-stock-of-asian-players (accessed Nov. 12, 2015).

Chapter 4. Ichigaga!

1. Robert Whiting, *The Meaning of Ichiro: The New Wave From Japan and the Transformation of Our National Pastime* (New York: Hachette, 2004). E-book.
2. Valerie Reitman, "Special Export?" *Los Angeles Times*, Nov. 11, 2000, ProQuest.
3. Ibid.
4. Ibid.
5. John Henderson, "Japanese Juggernaut," *Denver Post*, Mar, 14, 2001, ProQuest.
6. Judith Levin, *Ichiro Suzuki* (New York: Chelsea House, 2007), p. 59.
7. Ibid.
8. "A Look Back: Preseason Predictions," *ESPN.com*, Nov. 9, 2001, http://assets.espn.go.com/mlb/s/2001/1109/1275989.html (accessed Nov. 17, 2015).
9. Stephen Hawkins, "Ichiro's Homer Beats A-Rod's Rangers," *Columbian*, Apr. 7, 2001, ProQuest.
10. David Shields, "Being Ichiro," *New York Times*, Sept. 16, 2001, http://www.nytimes.com/2001/09/16/magazine/being-ichiro.html?pagewanted=all (accessed Nov. 18, 2015).
11. Ibid.
12. "10 Burning Questions for Ichiro Suzuki," *ESPN.com*, 2001, https://espn.go.com/page2/s/questions/ichiro010507.html (accessed Nov. 18, 2015).
13. Jim Cour, "Mariners' Celebration Likely Will Be Subdued," *Columbian*, Sept. 15, 2001, ProQuest.
14. Ibid.

15. Rod Beaton, "Suzuki Wins AL MVP Honors," *USA Today*, Nov. 11, 2001, http://usatoday30.usatoday.com/sports/baseball/stories/2001-11-20-al-mvp.htm (accessed Nov. 21, 2015).
16. Rob Dibble, "Eating Crow, Thanks to Ichiro," *ESPN.com,* Oct. 4, 2001, http://espn.go.com/talent/danpatrick/s/2001/1004/1259399.html (accessed Nov. 21, 2015).

Chapter 5. Hit Machine

1. Jeanne Lang Jones, "Tourism Groups Pitch M's Ichiro," *Puget Sound Business Journal*, Apr. 12, 2002, ProQuest.
2. Wayne Coffey, "Saying Sayonara," *New York Daily News*, Jan. 6, 2002, ProQuest.
3. Michael Berardino, "No Sophomore Slump for Ichiro," *Knight Ridder Tribune News Service,* June 3, 2002, ProQuest.
4. Ibid.
5. S. L. Price, "The Ichiro Paradox," *SI.com,* July 8, 2002, http://www.si.com/vault/2002/07/08/326024/the-ichiro-paradox-no-power-no-personality-yet-with-no-peer-the-mariners-ichiro-suzuki-may-be-the-greatest-player-to-come-out-of-japan-and-the-worst-thing-to-happen-to-japanese-baseball (accessed Nov. 24, 2015).
6. Ken Daley, "Ichiro Shows No Signs of Slowdown," *Knight Ridder Tribune News Service,* July 22, 2002, ProQuest.
7. Ross Newhan, "Around the Horn," *Los Angeles Times*, Sept. 22, 2002, ProQuest.
8. Jim Caple, "Ichiro's Bats More Than Pieces of Wood," *ESPN.com,* July 1, 2002, http://a.espncdn.com/mlb/

columns/caple_jim/1400915.html (accessed Nov. 25, 2015).

9. Ibid.
10. John Hickey, "Mariners 8, Angels 4: Ichiro, Boone Slam Angels," *Seattle Post-Intelligencer*, June 17, 2003, http://www.seattlepi.com/news/article/Mariners-8-Angels-4-Ichiro-Boone-slam-Angels-1117364.php (accessed Nov. 27, 2015).
11. Larry Stone, "Inside Pitch: Ichiro Explained in New Book," *Seattle Times*, May 2, 2004, http://old.seattletimes.com/html/sports/2001917747_ston02.html (accessed Nov. 27, 2015).
12. Larry LaRue, "Mariners' Debacle Halfway Over," *Spokesman Review*, July 7, 2004, ProQuest.
13. Thomas Stinson, "Ichiro Suzuki: Hitting Machine," *Atlanta Journal-Constitution*, Aug. 22, 2004, ProQuest.
14. Ibid.
15. Timothy Egan, "Mariners Realize the Value of Ichiro," *Toronto Star*, Oct. 3, 2004, ProQuest.
16. Les Carpenter, "The Hit King Stays Guarded," *Washington Post*, May 24, 2005, ProQuest.
17. Ibid.
18. Associated Press, "Vocal Ichiro Reports to Mariners' Camp," *Columbian*, Mar. 8, 2006, ProQuest.
19. Larry LaRue, "'So Many Things Out There,' and Ichiro Gets One," *Knight Ridder Tribune Business News,* June 6, 2006, ProQuest.

Chapter 6. Battles in Seattle

1. Jon Saraceno, "Ichiro Changes Perspective," *USA Today*, May 16, 2007, ProQuest.

2. "Ichiro Hits an Inside-the-Park Home Run," YouTube video, posted by MLB, https://www.youtube.com/watch?v=OiwO2BjcweU.
3. Associated Press, "MVP Ichiro Hits All-Star Game's First Inside-the-Park Homer," *ESPN.com,* July 11, 2007, http://sports.espn.go.com/mlb/recap?gameId=270710132 (accessed Nov. 30, 2015).
4. Ibid.
5. Associated Press, "Mariners Sign Ichiro Through 2012 Season," *ESPN.com,* July 13, 2007, http://sports.espn.go.com/mlb/news/story?id=2935612 (accessed Nov. 30, 2015).
6. Gregg Bell, "Ichiro Greeted Like Hero but Disappoints the Kids," *Toronto Star*, May 9, 2008, ProQuest.
7. Ibid.
8. Ryan Divish, "When Ichiro Talks, Media Listens," *McClatchy-Tribune Business News*, Feb. 21, 2008, ProQuest.
9. Ibid.
10. Jim Caple, "President Gets Ball to Plate on the Fly," *ESPN.com,* July 14, 2009, http://espn.go.com/espn/print?id=4328439 (accessed Dec. 2, 2015).
11. David Brown, "Ichiro? 'Wee Chiro' Tops Keeler With 9th Straight 200-Hit," *Yahoo! Sports,* Sept. 13, 2009, http://sports.yahoo.com/mlb/blog/big_league_stew/post/Ichiro-Wee-Chiro-tops-Keeler-with-9th-straigh?urn=mlb,189139 (accessed Dec. 2, 2015).
12. STATS writer, "White Sox-Mariners Preview," *SportingNews.com,* Sept. 14, 2009, http://www.sportingnews.com/mlb-news/116745-white-sox-mariners-preview (accessed Dec. 3, 2015).

13. Associated Press, "Ichiro Is Depressed by Another Mariners Lost Season," *Charleston Daily Mail*, July 16, 2010, ProQuest.
14. John Hickey, "Griffey Retires from the Game He Loved," *Seattle PostGlobe.org*, June 2, 2010, http://seattlepostglobe.org/2010/06/02/mariners-win-one-for-griffey-as-he-retires-from-the-game-he-loved/ (accessed Dec. 3, 2015).
15. Larry Stone, "Ichiro Makes His Record-setting Hit Count for More Than Just Milestone in M's Win," *Seattle Times*, Apr. 2, 2011, http://www.seattletimes.com/sports/mariners/ichiro-makes-his-record-setting-hit-count-for-more-than-just-milestone-in-ms-win/ (accessed Dec. 4, 2015).
16. Larry Stone, "Ichiro Tries for Payback Homer on First Pitch," *Seattle Times*, July 15, 2009, http://www.seattletimes.com/sports/mariners/ichiro-tries-for-payback-homer-on-first-pitch/ (accessed Nov. 28, 2015).
17. Jerry Brewer, "Superhero Ichiro Showing His Mortality," *Vancouver Sun*, July 8, 2011, ProQuest.
18. Daniel Barbarisi, "Konnichiwa, Ichiro," *Wall Street Journal*, July 24, 2012, ProQuest.
19. Jerry Brewer, "Ichiro's Exit Saves Mariners Pain, Disappointment," *Seattle Times*, July 23, 2012, http://www.seattletimes.com/sports/ichiros-exit-saves-mariners-pain-disappointment/ (accessed Dec. 4, 2012).
20. Barbarisi.
21. Kevin Dowd, "For the Seattle Mariners, It's the End of the Ichiro Era," *Seattle Post-Intelligencer*, July 24, 2012, http://blog.seattlepi.com/baseball/2012/07/24/for-the-seattle-mariners-its-the-end-of-the-ichiro-era/ (accessed Dec. 5, 2015).

CHAPTER 7. 4,000 AND BEYOND

1. "Ichiro's First Hit as a Yankee," MLB.com video, July 23, 2012, http://m.mlb.com/video/topic/6479266/v23289655/nyysea-ichiro-singles-in-his-first-yankees-atbat.
2. Ibid.
3. Daniel Barbarisi, "Covering the Enigma That Is Ichiro," *Wall Street Journal*, Aug. 11, 2012, ProQuest.
4. Brad Lefton, "The Secret Gym of Ichiro Suzuki," *Wall Street Journal*, Mar. 5, 2013, ProQuest.
5. Andrew Marchand, "Ichiro Suzuki Reaches 4K-hit Plateau," *ESPN.com,* Aug. 22, 2013, http://espn.go.com/new-york/mlb/story/_/id/9589905/ichiro-suzuki-new-york-yankees-gets-4000th-professional-hit (accessed Dec. 6, 2015).
6. Joel Sherman, "On the Outs," *New York Post*, Mar. 13, 2014, ProQuest.
7. Juan C. Rodriguez, "Marlins' Ichiro, 41, Playing for More than 3,000 Hits," *South Florida Sun-Sentinel*, Feb. 25, 2015, ProQuest.
8. Craig Davis, "Ichiro's Dramatic Homer Ices Mets," *McClatchy-Tribune Business News*, Apr. 30, 2015, ProQuest.
9. Craig Davis, "Ichiro Shows His Stuff in Surprise Pitching Debut for Marlins," *McClatchy-Tribune Business News*, Oct. 5, 2015, ProQuest.
10. Author e-mail interview with Stuart Shea, Dec. 2, 2015.
11. Ibid.
12. Ibid., Dec. 7, 2015.

Glossary

breaking pitch—A pitch that does not travel straight, such as a curveball or a slider; a change-up is not a breaking pitch.

contract—A legal agreement between individuals or companies; those who sign it are required by law to adhere to its terms.

control pitcher—A pitcher who throws the ball where he or she wants to and rarely walks batters.

excruciating—In a great deal of pain.

gastric ulcer—A sore in the lining of the stomach, often caused by stress.

hazing—To subject a person to ridicule or harassment.

internment camp—A prison camp for enemies of the government; used primarily during wartime.

Islamic extremist—One who supports the use of violence for achieving the goals of Islam (the religion of Muslims).

loophole—An opportunity to evade a law or rule.

oxygenate—To enrich, combine, or treat with oxygen.

paparazzi—Freelance photographers who take pictures of celebrities in public (and often private) places.

prefecture—An administrative district of a country; only some countries have prefectures.

professor emeritus—A retired professor who still maintains an official association with his or her university.

sarcasm—Saying something opposite of its meaning in order to achieve humorous effect.

skipper—Another word for a baseball manager.

surname—Another word for a person's last name.

unorthodox—Done in an unusual and nontraditional way.

Further Reading

Books

Jacobs, Greg. *The Everything Kids' Baseball Book: From Baseball's History to Today's Favorite Players—With Lots of Home Run Fun in Between!* Avon, MA: Adams Media, 2014.

Komatsu, Narumi. *Ichiro on Ichiro*. Seattle: Sasquatch Books, 2004.

Shields, David. *Baseball Is Just Baseball: The Understated Ichiro.* New York: Penguin Group, 2012.

Smolka, Bo. *The Best MLB Outfielders of All Time.* Edina, MN: ABDO Publishing, 2014.

Taylor, Charlotte. *The Internment of Japanese Americans.* New York: Enslow Publishing, 2016.

Websites

Baseball-Reference.com

www.baseball-reference.com/players/s/suzukic01.shtml
You'll find statistics of every one of Ichiro's professional seasons, even in Japan.

ESPN.com

espn.go.com/mlb/player/_/id/4570/ichiro-suzuki
Besides featuring his statistics, this page includes links to videos and news articles related to Ichiro.

MLB.com

m.mlb.com/player/400085/ichiro-suzuki
Ichiro's MLB page.

Index